Beyond the Mirrors

A study of the mental and spiritual aspects of horsemanship

Jill Keiser Hassler

edited by *Jane Bartholomew*
illustrated by *Eleanor McDonald*

Third Printing, April 1994

Published by:
Goals Unlimited Press
162 Stuart Run Road
Quarryville, PA 17566

The author is grateful to the following publishers and individuals for their permission to reprint excerpts and share their ideas:

Bartholomew, Dr. Gilbert L., Adjunct Assistant Professor of New Testament, Lancaster Theological Seminary, Lancaster, PA. "St. Paul's First Letter to the Corinthians 13:4-8A., A paraphrase for competitors."

Cather, Willa, (1926), *Death Comes for the Archbishop*, Alfred A. Knopf, Inc.

I dedicate this book to:

Russell Scoop who provided the energy for this book through sharing his gift of healing

Scott Hassler who has shown through his performance and sportsmanship the use of these ideals

my students who have been inspirational teachers to me

and to Jane and Gil Bartholomew for their time, patience and inspiration.

Author's Note

Look deeply into yourself.
Look deeply into your horse.
Evaluate what you find.
Compare it to what you know.
Ask questions, especially, "Why?"
Practice each new thing until it is second-nature.
And, most of all, enjoy your horse and yourself!

"Beyond the Mirrors" could be the most important book you have yet read about horses! It will help you:

Better understand your horse, yourself and others;

Understand why you feel so good spending time with your horse, and why you can carry your happiness over into your "real" life;

Actually GAIN energy from your riding recreation;

Better understand the importance of communication with horse and man;

Make faster progress in your horsemanship; and

Develop your artistic talents with your horse.

In *"Beyond the Mirrors"* I will share with you what I have learned in my years of self-search, teaching and personal experiences. I hope that you will identify with some of the chapters, be inspired by others, and gain a deeper insight into your horsemanship and life from all. The result should be a happy and healthy rider and horse.

You may find "Resources for the Journey" and "The Journey to Beyond" easier to read than the introductory parts, because these two parts are more concrete. But, please don't skip the "Introduction" and "Two Creatures" completely, because they provide the philosophical and psychological background for my entire approach to horsemanship and life. They establish the framework upon which all of my ideas are developed and balanced.

Jill Keiser Hassler

Contents

The Journey to Beyond

Beyond the Mirrors

Preface

Look beyond the surface; look deeply within your horse and yourself. Being a horseman is more than just "knowing how to ride." Being a horseman implies finely-tuned communication between you and your horse. It implies that you are sufficiently at peace with yourself that you can maximize the natural beauty of the horse. You and your horse move with a grace and beauty that make you look as though you are one.

Many books already address the *physical* aspects of riding; but teaching the body how to balance and how to give the aids is just the first stage of horsemanship. Nevertheless, it is a critical and essential stage. The artistic qualities of fine horsemanship are not possible without a firm grounding in the basics. In fact, your seat, balance and aids must be so much a part of you that you no longer have to think about them. It is then that you can begin to create a picture of unity with your horse.

While your body is gaining riding skills, you are already entering the second stage of horsemanship. Your mind is developing both knowledge of the horse and insight into its own inner workings. Communication with the horse is heightened, marked by the ability to produce consistently the desired response. Horsemanship, then, becomes *mental* as well as physical. You come to understand how a horse's mind works and why he responds as he does. You may also acquire the mental ability to influence other ceatures. The ability learned through work with horses is transferable to human interactions. Given time, you may enter yet a third stage. You may begin to relate to the horse on an even deeper level. A unity may evolve, allowing a deep, natural communication between horseman and horse. For me, the unity is *spiritual*. It is an essential component for the free natural movement of the horse when mounted. It is marked by the maximization of the horse's potential for natural beauty and the development of the rider's "inner-harmony."

I think of "inner-harmony" and unity between horse and rider as gifts. The gifts are available to everyone who is open to the patient search for knowledge required to understand the balance between the body, mind and spirit. A horseman cannot teach himself "inner-harmony." He cannot create unity between himself and his horse by the way he sits in the saddle or gives the aids. He can only prepare himself so that he will recognize "inner-harmony" and unity as they come.

"Inner-harmony" and unity between horse and rider may seem unreachable goals for many riders. However, their elusiveness does not eliminate the value of the search. They may emerge during the pursuit of other goals. The personal resources and horsemanship skills that are developed along the road are important in themselves. The horseman can become more completely in control of his own emotions, attitudes, and destiny and the horse can become more beautiful and trusting. All of these are desirable goals in their own right.

As an ultimate goal, the spiritual unity between horse and rider would reveal the full beauty of the horse as a living creature. Each horse has a natural beauty in temperament, body and movement, if he is unhindered by poor training, poor handling or poor riding. My goal as a rider, trainer, handler and instructor is to release this natural beauty to its fullest extent. Achieving this beauty for all to enjoy is the result of building spiritual unity between the human and the horse.

My goal as a person is to approach my own life with the same positive attitude, commitment, energy, and love as I approach my horses. I must accept myself, but never stop growing. I must develop myself spiritually to be prepared for the ultimate relationship I am seeking with my horse. The sense of personal peace I come to feel I call "inner-harmony."

"Inner-harmony" is the result of balance in my life. Balance is a critical concept and it exists on many levels in horsemanship. First, the horse must be physically balanced through his conformation to do the job expected of him. Second, the rider must be in balance with the horse's motion. Third, the balance of the body, mind and spirit of each being individually is necessary for learning and growth. Fourth, the balance of body, mind and spirit of both beings together is necessary for developing spiritual unity between horse and rider.

Huge mirrors are found in many indoor riding halls. They permit the rider to see his own form and that of his horse while schooling. But the rider must journey beyond the image he sees in the mirror in search of his "inner-harmony" and a spiritual unity between himself and his horse. It is only when he finds it that the image can approach perfect beauty and harmony.

In this book I will advise you on how to find a good instructor to help you develop the motor skills necessary for good horsemanship. I will make suggestions to develop your mental and spiritual resources so that you can communicate more accurately, sensitively, and consistently with your horse and your peers. And I will guide your attitudes toward life in a way that can lead to "inner-harmony" and a sense of unity between you and your horse. Then, given a glimpse of what lies beyond the mirror, you will be able to recognize the gift if it is received.

Goals

Introduction

W hatever your reason for riding, be it exercise, therapy, recreation, business, challenge, self-development, or a search for inner-harmony, you will receive more enjoyment and fulfillment by setting goals for yourself and your horse. As you reach your goal you will be able to praise yourself for a job well done. Recognition of your accomplishment gives you the incentive to advance further with your horse, or it can give you the self-confidence you need to overcome difficulties in your social, business or personal relationships. Without a goal you cannot realize when you are successful.

Goal-setting forms the backbone of the commitment you must make to care for your horse. Horses involve a large commitment in terms of money and time and without a goal, the commitment might fade. Your horse could suffer from lack of feed and water, poor medical care or inadequate exercise. You could suffer though perhaps unconsciously: Recognizing your horse's lack of care, but unmotivated to do anything about it, you can grow increasingly dissatisfied with yourself as a caretaker and, ultimately, as a person.

Growth toward your goals is not possible without some struggle and difficulty. In facing the difficulties you will have to choose where to place the blame. Obvious choices include your horse, your instructor, the bad weather, or the relationship between yourself and your horse. When honest self-examination leads **you to take responsibility** for the situation and seek improvement, you will grow. Each day will then bring you closer to your goal.

Pursuing a goal with your riding can have many positive effects. At the very least, your experience with horses should bring you many happy memories. Many college students feel their years with horses helped them be more responsible students. Parents often admit that their years with horses helped them deal effectively with their children. Those employed find that their relationship with horses prepared them to have harmonious relationships with their co-workers.

Take a mirror and hold it up in front of yourself. What are you looking for? Are you content to see a handsome face or do you want to see something more? Do you want to see the same image every day, or do you want to see changes? In what direction do you want your image to change? Do you want to understand the mind and spirit that make that face live? Should that mind and spirit be changed in any way? By answering these questions you will be identifying your goals. Then you can set the mirror aside and try to reach your goals. After a time, as you look in the mirror you will be able to recognize and reward yourself for your progress. But without identifying the goal you would not be able to measure the results of your striving.

Physical Goals

*I*f your reason for riding is exercise, therapy, recreation, or business, your goals may be primarily physical ones. You may seek to improve your image in the mirror by sharpening such physical skills as balance, suppleness, muscle tone and correctness of the aids. Or, you may seek simply to enjoy the physical activity offered by riding or working with horses.

To be healthy, your body needs exercise. Horseback riding can be physically exerting or pleasingly restful. The choices are as varied as riding a bucking horse in a rodeo or taking a trail ride in the country. The sport offers enough options to fit anyone's need for exercise.

Even a modest commitment to horseback riding can be beneficial. Mary was an athletic young woman who worked with computers full time. Her job kept her behind a desk, but she wanted exercise and she loved animals and the out of doors. Horseback riding through the countryside met her needs and fit in her schedule. Her initial goal was to ride three days a week, after work when weather and light permitted and on weekends. As she met her goal with trail riding, Mary felt better and she decided to expand her riding. She learned about competitive trail riding and how she would have to better condition herself and her horse. Her next goal was to prepare for a ten-mile ride. Because of her work schedule, preparation for the ride was spread out over many weeks. As her horse became more fit, Mary found that she felt more fit, too. She felt more attractive in her work clothes and she received comments from her fellow workers about her new vitality and attractiveness.

Riding is one of the more enjoyable forms of physical therapy. The warmth and companionship of the horse help with motivation. The horse's conformation and movement gently stretch tight muscles and improve balance. Riding helps in the regeneration of muscles that were forced to be inactive during the process of bone healing. Patients with muscular dystrophy find range-of-motion exercises easier and less painful with regular riding. Riding is recognized as such effective therapy that some hospitals in England maintain horses and riding programs as part of their service to patients.

Horseback riding is a fun way to spend leisure time. Horses provide a chance to be in the fresh air of the country. The motion of the horse can be relaxing to tired muscles and soothing to overworked minds. Action, thrills and excitement are possible with many forms of horse sport. Horseback riding provides the partnership of another living creature, yet allows a choice between solitude or group interaction.

As a business, horses provide various options for being physically active and out of doors. Physically rewarding ways to work with horses include riding and training professionally, being a groom, a veterinarian, or a farrier.

A friend returning from a long day in the hunt field remarked: "This day's hunt made my five days in the courtroom worthwhile. I will sleep without break for ten hours and be ready for another week in the courtroom!"

Mental
and
Spiritual
Goals

P erhaps you are one of the few for whom the reason for
riding is the challenge, self-development, or search for
inner-harmony. If so, you probably have found the physical
rewards of horsemanship and are looking for a deeper relationship or challenge. You may recognize that horses can help
you grow mentally and spiritually and realize that any further
improvement to the image in your mirror will have to come
from within.

If so, this book is written especially for you. It is a guide
for your development with your horse beyond the mechanics
of correct position and use of the aids and beyond the physical
benefits of exercise and relaxation. But the book should also
be a challenge to those who ride primarily for the physical
benefits. So much more enjoyment of the horse is possible if
the rider expands his goals to include those of mental and
spiritual growth. What a shame not to explore the potential.

Riding with the goals of mental and spiritual growth is not
limited to a select few. Consider the story of Amy. Amy was
a fifteen year old high school drop-out. She had many personal problems and was very depressed. Life had little or no
meaning. The only emotions Amy showed were hate and
anger. She hated school, authority and life. Years before her

depression began she had a horse she loved to ride. Together with a psychologist, I developed a program for Amy. Naturally, we wanted her to overcome the depression, graduate from school and find happiness in life. Amy's love of horses was the only positive ingredient we had to work with, so our first step was to reinstate riding lessons. By praising her positive attributes we were able to build her self-esteem and motivate her further. Gradually the moments on horseback became time free of depression; brightness developed. After a couple of weeks, as Amy became more in tune with her horse, we began to discuss life and responsibilities.

We addressed real-life problems, including her performance at school. School was such a trauma that Amy daily became physically ill. The school and I stood firm. We resisted her illness and forced her to remain in school. Although there were many months of strong-willed confrontations, Amy's riding continued to improve. Her horse life proved that success was possible. She had success in her training, successful competitions, up-gradings in the United States Pony Club. Gradually her school problems decreased.

Amy is now a successful person. She is fully employed in industry and trains and rides horses as an avocation. She graduated from college with honors, a long way from the high school drop-out.

What gave Amy the chance? Her strong character and her willingness to accept fair authority helped, but primarily it was her love of horses in general which gave her the desire and energy to learn and grow with horses. Her attitude was positive only when working with horses. Success with her horse developed her self-esteem enough to face school. The commitment to her horse and her goals gave her a reason to live. The spiritual unity Amy developed with her horse brought her comfort and inner-harmony. Inner-harmony gave her the strength to overcome adversity. She confronted her problems instead of avoiding them.

What was the comfort offered by the horse? When you love horses there is an unconditional bond between both beings. The horse accepts you as you are; when you recognize the acceptance you lose the loneliness resulting from personal fears. The spiritual unity Amy felt is with her to this day. She experiences personal peace when in the presence of a horse. Amy is not unique. At some time in our lives, all of us have felt negativism and depression similar to Amy's. If you are a horseman, your riding will improve and your horse will be happier if you can find peace with yourself. Conversely, your relationship with your horse can help you cope with your fears and ambitions. As with Amy, your life with horses can be both the means and the reward of successful personal growth.

Amy achieved inner-harmony through her riding. She started out trying to overcome depression but ended with inner-harmony. You, too, may begin with a less ambitious goal. If you like to overcome challenges, horses can be highly instructive. Facing a challenge may make you tense, but horses give a warm, unconditional love that allows you to relax. The more relaxed you are, the more you can concentrate on defining the problem. You may need to do some research to get the answer to the problem. Implementation involves thoroughly understanding the horse. Horses have simple minds that receive our communications exactly as they are given, and they react accordingly. If you vacillate, your horse will not know how to respond. The horseman must learn to speak precisely, immediately, and softly. The horse will not hold a grudge; he responds only to the present communication. He demonstrates how to forget past problems. Successful practice meeting challenges with your horse can give you a model to apply to meeting other challenges in your life.

Another goal could be to develop yourself further in a specific area of weakness. It could be making yourself more patient, or more relaxed, or improving your concentration, or self-discipline. Any of these personal goals can be addressed through your riding. Your relationships with both horses and people will improve as a result of meeting your personal goals for self-improvement.

The mental and spiritual aspects of your relationship with your horse are all related. Developing yourself in one area will carry over into others. Also, developing yourself in relation to your horse will affect your relationship with people. Your conscious or unconscious desire to balance your body, mind and spirit will help to motivate you. Consequently, you may find that what started out as a limited goal of self-improvement has expanded into a wider search for inner-harmony, as happened to Amy. I encouraged her to ride to bring a positive ingredient into her depressed life but she enlarged her goals and grew with them as she journeyed beyond her mirror.

Look into YOUR mirror — and beyond. List your goals for yourself and for your horsemanship. As you put them into a workable order be realistic and flexible. Seek professional help, if appropriate. Commit yourself to meeting the goals one at a time. Do not expect miracles, but do expect steady growth. Reward yourself each time you achieve one of your goals. You should be able to see your advancement in the image of your mirror. Your journey of self-discovery will never end, however. You will continue to travel as long as you live.

Two
Creatures

Introduction

The fact that you and your horse are such different creatures adds an extra level of difficulty to any artistic statement you make together. The demands on you are beyond those made on two humans dancing a *pas de deux* or playing tennis. In body, *you* are relatively small and weak, but in mind "intelligent." In body *your horse* is heavy and powerful, but in mind less "intelligent." Spiritually you and your horse are also different. If *you*, the rider, are typical of a person brought up in Western culture, you are oriented to the future, you are seeking some form of personal growth (more possessions, greater knowledge, more highly respected character), and you are seeking to exercise some form of control over your environment to improve upon what nature or society has given you to start with. *Your horse*, on the other hand, lives in the present, is content with himself, what he knows, and whatever food and water and stabling he happens to have, as long as these things are reasonably adequate. All these contrasts make the achievement of communication and unity with your horse very remarkable, and in my opinion far more remarkable than communication and unity between two human beings. No matter to what level of horsemanship you aspire, you must understand not only your own human characteristics but also the very different characteristics of your horse. And the more you understand yourself and your horse, the more you will enjoy each other.

People have little difficulty recognizing and accepting the differences in physical structure between man and horse. But the differences in mind and spirit are often either unknown or ignored. We frequently assign human characteristics to our horse's mind and spirit instead of accepting our horse on his own terms. Doing this is unfair to the horse. It robs him of his special identity, and it prevents us from enjoying our horse to the fullest. Journeying beyond the mirrors requires understanding both the human and equine minds and spirits as well as their physical make-up. And so I shall give an extended picture of these differences in the two chapters which follow.

What I am going to say about people and horses I have learned from my own experience of working with troubled teenagers and teaching riding to both handicapped and "normal" youth and adults. I have had a great deal of opportunity to observe both man and horse as they interact with each other and to guide people in their search for greater and more fruitful understanding both of their horses and of themselves. I am not pretending to be an experimental psychologist offering scientifically tested conclusions. As you read these pages you may say, "I'm not like that. I wouldn't react that way." And I will respond, "Good! These notes are from *my* experience. Analyze yourself and identify your responses and relationships. It is by learning to know yourself that you will grow, not by memorizing what I have to say."

When I use the term "spirit," I do so because, as I have worked with both people and horses, it has become very clear to me that there is another dimension to both the human and the equine make-up that is not adequately covered by speaking of the "body" and the "mind." When I use the word "spiritual," I am referring to basic *attitudes* and *aspirations* in the two different creatures in contrast to particular mental operations to which they may lead. For example, the horse is capable of accepting an incredible amount of human control. A human being, on the other hand, is capable of developing

14

a profound respect for the character, abilities, and limitations of a particular horse. A human being is capable of accepting them as a given and of working with them in order to bring out the best that particular horse has to offer. The horse's willingness and the human's respect and acceptance are non-physical in character, but they are very real. So are other attitudes and aspirations of both man and horse, as well as the *relationship between man and horse* which they may produce. All these things — attitudes, aspirations, and relationships — as well as particular mental operations, are, of course, firmly rooted in the workings of the body. But they themselves are not physical and they must be clearly distinguished from the physical. Beyond that, they have a reality which we can appropriately label "spiritual." They may even be manifestations of a reality beyond the physical, and unlike the body they may be eternal and not just temporary. But that is a matter of faith. What is important here is to recognize that they exist and to learn that they play an essential role in horsemanship.

In my introduction to the attitudes and aspirations of humans, I said that my description applied to you "if you are typical of a person brought up in Western culture." People brought up in other cultures approach life and the world in a different way. For example, Willa Cather, in *Death Comes for the Archbishop,* contrasts the Indian and European ways:

> They seemed to have none of the European's desire to "master" nature, to arrange and re-create. They spent their ingenuity in the other direction; in accommodating themselves to the scene in which they found themselves. This was not so much from indolence, the bishop thought, as from inherited caution and respect. It was as if the great country were asleep, and they wished to carry on their lives without awakening it; or as if the spirits of earth and air and water were things not to antagonize and arouse.

In riding a horse, it is important not only to become knowledgable about our own spiritual and mental characteristics, but to discover alternatives that can be learned from other cultures.

For example, we may wish to retain our Western aspiration to reach new heights in our horsemanship skills and to improve upon what horses naturally do in the wild, and if we do we will find it very useful to use the highly developed ability for analysis we have inherited from our Western culture. But if we are going to arrive at our goal, we shall also have to give up certain parts of our Western inheritance and to develop some new mental skills. We shall have to give up our inclination to control our horse by force. Instead we shall have to try to learn and then to respect the way *he* wants to do things, and then use our superior intelligence to get him to do what *we* want *his way*. And, instead of trying to impose on our particular animal our idea of what he should be able to achieve, we must first seek to learn what his capabilities really are, and then be accepting enough to bring those to new heights instead of insisting that he try to do other things. Beyond that, we shall have to add to our analytical capability an equal capacity for intuitive thought. Without this new spiritual and mental equipment, our relationship with our horse will be one of spiritual warfare instead of harmony and beauty.

Man

A mong members of the animal kingdom, man is not noted for his *physical* prowess. He is not particularily strong, nor fast, nor are his teeth very sharp. It is his mind and spirit that set him apart from other creatures. His mind and spirit allow him to become a horseman — to become patient, courageous, humble, self-disciplined, consistent, and aware — to teach the horse and to learn from the horse. Man's mental and spiritual qualities have made it possible for him to use his physical skills of balance and coordination to ride the horse for pleasure or work, war or show.

Man's *mind* gives him the opportunity to do so much with his world. It can master thousands of facts, understand complex scientific formulae, engage in flights of creative fantasy, or explore the meaning of the universe. Yet the mind can also be a handicap. Its very talents can interfere with man's abiltiy to relate to other creatures, either human or equine. The rational, logical, verbal, educated aspect of man's mind overrides his sensitive, intuitive nature, which is the part of him that is aware of other people's feelings, his horse's attitudes, the music of birds, or the beauty of a dance.

Few people really balance the two ways of using their minds. Some prefer to be analytical because in this way they feel more in control. Others tend to be reactive, responding to their feel for what is right. Most of us tend toward the former approach. We overlook body language and other signs of someone's true feelings because we are concentrating on the subject under discussion. We tend to avoid our inner feelings and intuition and concentrate on our analytical thinking. But our horses can neither think this way nor communicate verbally. To relate to them most effectively we must learn to use our intuition and be constantly aware of their signals.

Describing the mind in terms of its analytical/intuitive bias helps to explain why some people are better mathematicians and others are better with animals. A person who is more analytical may be able to explain the techniques of riding more effectively (a verbal skill requiring reasoning ability), whereas a person who is more intuitive may acquire his horse's trust more quickly (a non-verbal skill requiring awareness and feel). A truly efffective person will **balance both skills.** Achieving balance requires self-analysis and change, because everyone starts out learning one way or the other.

Another aspect of our nature is that we have both conscious and unconscious levels of our mind. The conscious level makes us aware of our experiences while we are experiencing them. At this level we process facts, analyze problems, recognize our feelings, explain reasons, memorize courses, and try to perform as we have been taught. Although the conscious mind is primarily controlled by our intellect, it is influenced by our race, culture, education, religion, family and life experiences. These influences may enhance or jeopardize our ability to function. Our intelligence gives us the chance to examine all of them and to change those that interfere with our riding or our life.

In the unconscious level of our mind we store data or react to stimuli of which we are not aware. In the unconscious level we may remember information we read, remember the mood of a certain piece of music, remember how it felt to do a flying change of lead, or remember fear in a certain circumstance. If asked to describe or explain one of these memories, we would not be able to do so. Yet the memory is true and may affect us physically. For example, suppose as a small child you fell and broke your leg. While unconscious and in shock you heard the ambulance siren. The result might be that, as an adult, you feel pain in your leg every time you hear a siren.

A balance between the two levels of consciousness is necessary for horsemanship. You will learn the proper use of the aids and remember them consciously, but to rehearse them mentally each time you want to communicate with your horse will destroy your timing. By not trying so hard, you can allow your unconscious mind to move your body in the correct and rhythmical manner necessary to communicate with the horse. All you need to do is to think of the results you want to produce, the way it will feel, and your body will do what is necessary. Learning has taken place on both the conscious and unconscious levels. Neither could function alone.

Everyone develops protections from real or imagined criticisms and tries to mold himself to the standards of society. This is a natural result of being part of a society. Nevertheless these techniques discourage us from recognizing our true selves and hinder us from relating honestly to other people or animals. Society encourages us not to let our true selves show. Showing our feelings is considered weak or in poor taste. Consequently, we tend to hide any sense of inadequacy or fear of performing from ourselves as well as from others. No matter how good we are at pretending or hiding, it is not possible to eliminate our feelings. We are always storing them in the unconscious level of our minds, beyond our control. However, our feelings do not change and they re-emerge occasionally to affect our relations with people or our performance on a horse.

When we do not examine our feelings we are being dishonest with ourselves. We can never heal after a real or imagined hurt until we recognize the facts. We seldom forget, when we have been hurt by another person emotionally. We are reluctant to confront the other person to learn if the hurt was intentional or caused by our faulty perception. Good manners preserve our socially acceptable behavior, but our trust may never again be complete. On a conscious level we respond as society has taught us by seeking retaliation, or refusing to be placated, and we fail to recognize the need for peaceful relations that may exist on an unconscious level. It takes considerable mental strength and work to be honest with ourselves and find out the truth.

Balancing for yourself both sets of contrasting aspects of your mind will take honest self-appraisal. It is not easy and may require some form of professional assistance. Learn from your horse. He has a much simpler response to life than you do. His mind is not clouded by attempts to conform to society. Your horse will greet you eagerly in the morning even though you punished him for not jumping yesterday. Not only does his acceptance of you help you to accept yourself, but also his unconditional love can guide you in establishing a loving, trusting, forgiving relationship with other humans.

The third, but most important aspect of our being is the *spirit*. Our spirit includes the attitudes and aspirations that lead us to act as we do. It involves our drive to improve ourselves, our love, our trust, our capacity for commitment. It is more than what we "know." It determines what we shall know.

In our Western tradition, we frequently equate our desire to grow (a spiritual quality) with a desire for being in charge of our world. We want to make the world better instead of accepting it as it is. We consider it better to be a leader than to be a follower. Yet leadership can easily turn into domination, and humility and the sense of proportion are lost. Any reluctance to control is thought of as a weakness. But in horsemanship, attempts to dominate the horse lead to loss of control over him. The horse is sensitive and objects to being bossed around. The successful horseman is one who can convince the horse that he wants to do what the trainer wants him to do. The trainer gives up his own nature and becomes what that horse needs at that moment. The trainer seeks the horse's cooperation and remains constantly aware of the horse's response. He never seeks to dominate the horse yet, in the end, the horse obeys his every wish. Rather than distorting his spirit by attempting to turn himself into a god, the wise horseman has accepted the horse on his own terms and enhanced both their spirits by what they have learned together.

Although I am suggesting that you can find spiritual unity with your horse, I do not think it is something that you can do consciously, or at will. Rather, by freeing yourself of mental and physical obstacles, your spirit will become able to merge with that of your horse. You must work, not to find spiritual unity with your horse, but to make yourself ready for it when it comes. In Resources for the Journey, I will help you develop good physical and mental habits for horsemanship. In The Journey to Beyond I will help you recognize and use those spiritual values important to horsemanship and life. How you use these resources and values will be up to you and your own urge to journey beyond your mirror.

Horse

A horse's *body* is designed for strength and speed. His survival in the wild depends on his athletic abilities, his alertness, his agility, his stamina. Left alone, a horse will move forward freely, gracefully, in balance and with natural beauty. Yet, with proper training, the horse is capable of even more grace and beauty than he exhibits in the wild. He can be taught to run faster, jump higher, turn shorter, and move with more controlled balance and impulsion.

The horse's *mind* is not as important to his survival as is his body. Brain power is more critical to predatory species than to those preyed upon. A horse has no reasoning ability. He is incapable of understanding why he is being treated in a certain way. He cannot understand a confinement to rest an injured leg.He might see it as boring, fearful, or uncomfortable, but not as therapeutic. If he unlatches the gate, it is not because he has analyzed the latch mechanism, but because of trial and error and considerable motivation.

Since the horse cannot reason, he learns by being sensitive to activities in his environment and by repetition and reward. He cannot generalize. He cannot know that brightly painted jumps are safe just because naturally colored ones are. He will jump them because he has learned they will not hurt him or because he trusts you not to ask him to do anything dangerous. If the horse does not do what you ask, it is probably because he is inattentive or unclear about your signals, not because he is stupid. The horse can respond only to the signals he feels; he cannot figure out what you really want. On the other hand, horses are notoriously quick to pick up signals from body language or to sense fear or danger. No matter how hard the human tries to hide his feelings, the horse senses them. On the positive side, the horse is equally quick to recognize a person who can relate to him.

In his video tape *Concepts of Dressage*, Charles DeKunffey talked about, ''The rider's mind in flight on the horse's legs.'' It is the horse's simple, accepting *spirit* that makes him an ideal vehicle for man to use to produce these wonderful physical performances. Why is the horse willing to do so much for us? What is special in his nature that we can learn from? Answering these questions will teach us how to relate to the horse so that he can learn willingly and perform eagerly, always improving his inherent talents and beauty.

A horse does not question the reasons for his existence. He accepts his place in the world as it comes to him. He doesn't try to hide his true feelings from other horses, rationalize his failures, or pretend to be what he is not. If another horse or person injures or punishes him, he may change his behavior, but he won't hold a grudge. The horse demonstrates an unconditional love toward those who care for him. He lives in the present, taking each moment as it comes. The horse's needs are modest and his mind is simple, straightforward and easy to understand.

In the wild, the horse accepts his position as part of a hierarchy. If that means he must wait behind several other bands at the water hole, then so be it. His only concerns are to eat, drink, sleep, procreate, and avoid predators. It is his nature to be part of a band. Roaming in search of grass is pleasurable for him and he accepts his position in a domestic scene with equal equanimity. Nevertheless, his real pleasures in life are his opportunities to behave as he would in the wild. Notice how sour horses who have raced or shown too much can be refreshed by a period at grass just "being like a horse."

To anyone who can read the signals, it is readily apparent whether a horse is eager or fearful, playful or aggressive. A horse does not hide his true nature behind a false exterior. Likewise he does not try to rationalize his behavior to avoid embarrassment. In training your horse you learn yourself because his response will always be straightforward and honest. You will be able to tell whether your aids were clear and consistent by the quality of his responses.

Just as the wild horse accepts his place in the hierarchy, the domesticated horse will accept you as his handler. Once he recognizes that you are a dependable authority, he will respect your corrections and alter his behavior accordingly. He never holds a grudge nor shows any resentment toward you for being his superior. Rather, he makes every effort to please you. You, in return, should adapt your training methods to promote freedom and pleasure for the horse to replace the natural pleasures that man has denied him.

The horse's efforts to please are not bought with carrots and lumps of sugar. Although the quality of care you give your horse may affect his trust in you, it will not alter his basic desire to do what you want. Only fear, or your failure to be in control, will diminish that desire. The desire to please allows the horse to overlook your social inadequacies and personal failures. He accepts you with an unconditional love.

Do not be misled by the foregoing generalities into believing that all horses are alike. Horses are as individual as are people. One of the joys of working with horses is the constant variety. It challenges the trainer's ingenuity and sensitivity to find solutions to each horse's own problems. There are obvious differences among horses in conformation and athletic ability. Mentally, too, there are great differences. One horse may learn the distance after just one trip through a jumping lane; another may be constantly inquisitive about activities in his barn. Spiritually, a horse may be gentle, kind and honest, or he may be a nasty bully. The horse is born with some personality traits; others evolve as he interacts with other horses and humans. Nevertheless, the horse's capabilities are shaped by the nature of his body, mind and spirit and they set the framework within which you, as his trainer, must operate. The important thing is to accept the horse on his own terms and not to expect him to behave like a human with four legs and a tail.

Resources
for
the
Journey

Introduction

W hen you look beyond the mirrors into yourself, you will see both your strengths and your weaknesses. Recognizing and accepting your strengths will allow you to capitalize on them and grow. Recognizing and accepting your weaknesses will allow you to overcome them.

"Resources for the Journey" helps you develop the horsemanship and living skills necessary to maintain what is good within you and to correct what you find to be deficient. To some extent, these skills are *physical*, but all are approached through your *mental* and *spiritual* faculties. They are the resources I have identified through my teaching and working with teenagers. They have helped me go beyond my mirror in my own search for inner-harmony.

Knowledge

*Whether you are a beginner or an expert,
a rider or an instructor, seek knowledge continually.*

*T*he mechanics of riding and training, the use of the aids, the rider's position, conditioning the horse — all these topics are covered widely in current and classical literature. Read as much as you can; discuss new ideas with your instructor or with someone else you respect; when you are sure you understand, try them. Your horse will tell you whether or not you are doing things correctly.

Select your teachers carefully. Learn from the best.

Knowledge

It is important to have an instructor, someone knowledge-able in your type of riding and with whom you feel comfort-able. Even if you are a proficient rider, you will need a ground person to provide you with feedback.

Choose carefully the instructors from whom to take clinics and the riders to observe. Require evidence of qualifications. Look for the instructor's own success over a period of time and look for the success of the instructor's students. What is suc-cess? One criterion is the number of horses and riders trained and their progression through competitive levels. The quality of the competitions is more important than the prizes won. Evaluate fairly, considering the capabilities of each horse and rider as well as the circumstances. Look for ability to instruct on a level appropriate to you and your horse.

Select someone whose success has been demonstrated, rather than someone who only talks of past glories. Those who are truly qualified do not need to boast or give false impres-sions. Success is relative. Some consider themselves experts if they have trained one horse. Is that sufficient experience to satisfy you?

The American horse world is still very young. It is difficult for a newcomer to the sport to find valid information. Very little is documented and there are no formal credentials to con-sider. Therefore, it is important to be an educated critic.

Bruce Davidson is an example of an expert who has earned that title. He has evented successfully at advanced levels both nationally and internationally. Each year he brings two new horses along to the advanced level. He trains many different breeds. His horses stay sound and sane. He also has coached his students up to the advanced level. Bruce obviously is qualified through his actions to be an example to any prospec-tive event rider. Why has Bruce been able to do so much? Because he continues to learn.

Use your powers of observation when you look for an in-structor. Visit, take a sample lesson, observe the attitude of those working in the stable, check safety procedures, the con-dition of the horses, the tack and the facilities.

Ask questions:
   Names of horses trained and competed
   Names of riders coached
   Names and levels of competitions
   How instructor is keeping knowledge updated
   Instructor's background
   Length of time at this location
   How you feel after a lesson or two

Evaluate the instructor's ability to communicate, his compassion for horse and rider, his knowledge and his willingness to learn more.

Instruction must be received with an open mind. During your lesson forget the outside world and concentrate completely on the lesson and the horse. In addition to the words of the instructor, retain the feel of what you are doing, try to experience all dimensions of the subject.

Learn as much as you can from that instructor before moving on to another who will bring you even closer to your ultimate goal.

Learn to know yourself as you learn about horsemanship.

The mind and spirit govern the body. The amount of inner balance and harmony you attain affects the amount of body control you will achieve and thus the clarity and subtlety of your aids. It also affects your sense of proportion and helps you to keep your own achievements and those of your horse in perspective. All three aspects of your being must be developed together.

Observation

Careful observation will lead you forward most quickly.
The learning may be both conscious and unconscious.

O bservation of good horses and riders can be a useful
learning tool. Attend clinics or national competitions as
an observer. In 1983 I watched *Falstaff* give an outstanding performance in the *Prix St. George* at the national dressage competitions at Kansas City. He stood out for his natural beauty,
his free forward movement, his impulsion and his relaxation.
He displayed wonderfully those qualities which should be
maintained from training level to *Grand Prix*. While watching
Falstaff's performance I asked myself what went into his training to develop and maintain his magnificent gaits. How much
did the quality of the riding affect the performance? Where was
he trained? By pursuing these questions I learned that it is
possible to bring out the natural beauty of a horse through

proper training. In the past I had had only a partial understanding acquired from reading and studying pictures. I now had a moving picture in my mind of a trained and relaxed horse in motion. I had more information I could use to train others.

At a clinic with Gunnar Ostergaard my students watched many beautiful, free-moving horses perform flying changes. They watched the horses intensely and discussed what they saw. That evening one student came home and rode her four year old. She immediately began performing flying changes effortlessly. She learned how to perform the flying change by watching the horses at the clinic. The significance of this accomplishment is that "feel," rather than "mechanics," is so important to the success of a flying change. Her mind had absorbed the feel and timing for both the horse and the rider simply by observing. To this day she is able to perform flying changes without effort.

I have observed the development of a prominent junior rider from the time he was five years old. For many years he trailed after his mother to various horse activities up and down the East Coast. He seemed oblivious to horses, but part of him must have been absorbing what he saw and heard. A few months after seeing him playing with his trucks, I saw him at a D-1 pony club rally. I was astonished. On the cross country course he looked like a miniature of one of our top three-day riders who has an unmistakable style all his own. He has continued to make fast progress in both eventing and dressage. His development made me understand the significance of observation as a learning device.

"On hold"

*Learning to put information "on hold"
can free you to live in the present.*

I t is virtually impossible to concentrate on the present when your mind is cluttered with details. They intrude on your consciousness: "I mustn't forget to call home and ask the children to get something out of the freezer for dinner." "I wonder if Sam will remember to buy horse feed?"

An invaluable tool to my learning and productivity is a technique I call "on hold." I store information in either my conscious or unconscious mind to be used when I need it. "On hold" works for me in two distinct ways: recording new data and clearing my mind to concentrate on something else.

When I receive new data, I make sure I understand it completely, evaluate its relevance and confirm its application while I am in total concentration. Then I store it. For example, you may learn the aids to make your horse move laterally while teaching a young horse dressage. However, you now have taken up the sport of foxhunting and you seldom even think of dressage. One day, on a fast run, you see a ground hog hole dead ahead. Your reactive mind responds immediately to move your horse laterally away from the hole. Your knowledge of the aids, your ability to use them, and their immediate availability in your unconscious mind saved you from a nasty fall. You had the information "on hold" from lessons learned years before.

Another way to use "on hold" is to free my mind to concentrate on the present by putting aside, without forgetting, information from prior activities. Because I am involved in so many different activities, I frequently must jump from one to the other without being able to complete the first.

If I am working in the office and I must go to teach a lesson, I store the information from the office and empty my mind. During the lesson my student and his horse have my total attention. After the lesson I summarize and evaluate what happened, enabling me to put the entire lesson "on hold" until I next see the student. Back at the office, I pull forward what I previously had placed "on hold" and complete my unfinished tasks.

Using this technique requires total concentration. You must review whatever you wish to put "on hold" and consciously store it before you allow yourself to be distracted. If you need to keep the information "on hold" for a long time, it is helpful to review it occasionally to keep it fresh. Being able to use the "on hold" technique will allow you a more productive and higher quality experience with your horse.

Love

*Love is more than the possessive feeling toward your
own horse or family. Love is a moral position,
an approach to life. Yet the horse can teach you how
to interact with others in a loving way.*

I believe that the deepest qualities of love are best expressed
in a paraphrase of First Corinthians 13:

Love bears patiently the evil of other people;
the good of those who harm is the goal of love.

Love is not envious when others receive the praise;
it is not always blowing its own horn in order to get praise;
it does not flaunt the praise it does receive;
it does not maintain its own reputation by knocking others
down.

Love is not always looking out for Number One;
it does not get worked up when things don't go its way.

Love does not keep a record of another's poor performance;
it does not rejoice in other people's errors,
but it joins in applauding a job well done.

Love is limitless in its encouragement,
limitless in its faithfulness
limitless in its hope,
limitless in its perseverence.

Love never suffers defeat.

(St. Paul's First Letter to the Corinthians 13:4-8A. A paraphrase for competitors. Dr. Gilbert L. Bartholomew.)

I believe that all of humanity aspires to this type of love. Some have found it, others are still searching, and still others deny the importance of this deepest form of love. Developing a love for the horse is a beginning for those who find it difficult to love themselves, humanity, or God.

If love of humanity, God, or even yourself is a difficult concept for you, start by looking at your relationship to your own horse. You try to understand him as he is, not project human feelings and attitudes onto him. You care for him first, after a long ride, before you think of your own needs. You provide him with appropriate food, shelter and exercise, and not let him stand bored all day in an overgrazed paddock. These are all elements of love.

You also may learn from your horse how to live for the beauty of the moment and another being. Every time I enter my stable my horse greets me with eagerness. He thanks me for a pat on the neck by pricking his ears and putting a smile in his eye. He rewards me for a hack in the country by giving me a free forward gait. He is an example of the kind of spontaneous appreciation and communication that is often suppressed in human contacts.

Love

A horse can be a friend to those who feel isolated and afraid after a tragedy. The horse allows you to express your emotional upheaval by just being there and accepting. The horse does nothing but look at you with his soft eyes; he offers no words of advice, no suggestions for action. He is simply there, allowing you to express your emotion, which is the first step in dealing with your emotional upheaval. Love of your horse can bring a catharsis that might otherwise elude you.

Bonding between man and animal can promote physical, as well as spiritual, healing. This healing potential is clearly demonstrated through the handicapped riding program. Each week, handicapped riders leave behind their limitations of movement, their crutches, their wheelchairs, and mount their horses. Suddenly, the struggle of life expressed on their faces is replaced by smiles, reflecting the feelings of freedom, acceptance, warmth, respect, and unconditional love. It is natural. It is free. It is beautiful.

One horse in the handicapped riding program had been an event horse at the preliminary level. For several years he had competed successfully at major United States Combined Training Association events on the East Coast. In the handicapped program a severely brain-damaged girl rode him once a week. She had been injured in an automobile accident during her junior year in high school. She grew to love the horse. Her therapists believed that more frequent riding would be the best possible way to rehabilitate her body, so we retired the horse from eventing and made him available to her. The horse exhibited tremendous patience and understanding. He never shied. He never ran. He actually bonded with her deep love. Those of us who knew the horse got more joy out of seeing his sensitive care of this injured girl than out of seeing him win at events. When she began to ride she was barely able to care for her own needs. She walked very slowly with a limp, falling frequently. She had no sense of direction; she could not go fifty feet alone without getting lost. Now, six years later, she walks with only a small limp, has her own car and drives alone wherever she wishes. She even holds a full-time job and is self-sufficient. The six years of bonding with this horse opened the doors of life to her.

Love of one horse prepares you to love all horses. This new dimension means that you must learn to love horses that may have been spoiled or who may have less natural talent. Your ability to love and bond with the horse in general gives you the patience and understanding to improve the horse. In a sense, you become the healer for the horse, rather than the other way around.

The implications for love in horsemanship are best expressed by Waldemar Suenig, in *Horsemastership*. He identifies the three basic resources a rider must have: Love of the horse, mental equilibrium and energy. He states:

> Most important is love of the horse. It is the *leitmotif* that should underlie all our intercourse with the most lovable of creatures. A horse will overcome its inborn shyness and gain confidence, the fundamental condition for mutual understanding, with man whose love it feels. Subsequently, when strictness or punishment becomes necessary, the horse will know it was deserved for it has never suffered injustice or arbitrariness. It has been able to judge the rider's good nature by the fact that he was on the lookout, so to speak, for the slightest indication of responsiveness to his controls to find an opportunity to reward his horse, and that he was magnanimous in forgetting to punish when the mistake was due to clumsiness or inadequate understanding.

A horse immediately recognizes a person who possesses this loving approach to horses in general. He responds quickly with his trust, his energy and his body. The performance is beautiful, even though there has been little time for practice or getting to know one another.

Loving your horse can lead you to love yourself. Does your horse love and accept himself? Of course he does. He has no reason not to. Watch your horse. He eats for his pleasure, sleeps for his pleasure, enjoys his companions and gives to you unselfishly. Can you do this? Understanding these characteristics in your horse can help you toward self-acceptance. When you accept yourself, your attitude toward life becomes more positive. The more you accept and love yourself, the more humility you will have toward others and your horse; the more accurate your vision will be.

You can transfer the attitude of love, learned from horses, to the people around you. You should find that you can treat others in the same patient, positive and spontaneous way that you treat your horse. If you feel negative from lack of response on their part, go to your horse! The companionship of your horse will recharge your love for those around you. Likewise, the commitment you developed to horses in general should have taught you how to relate fairly, consistently and generously, even to those who may not be so lovable. You should have learned to find and encourage the good in others, even when they resist. The ability to love that you have developed should stand by you, even when everything else is going wrong. You have found the critical resource to your relations with horses, your acceptance of yourself, and your appreciation of humanity and of God.

Energy

*Think of horsemanship, not as a sport that depletes
your physical energy, but as an art that both
uses and creates mental and spiritual energy.*

O f the three forms of energy - physical, mental, and
spiritual - the physical energy is the least essential to
horsemanship. Your mental energy gives you the perseverance, patience and self-discipline to be diplomatic with your
horse. Your spiritual energy motivates your being and feeds
your desire to learn and grow.

Your physical energy is important only in that your
muscles need to be strong and supple enough to remain in
balance with your horse. Physical fitness is required, but too
much physical energy in riding can limit the movement and
beauty of the horse. Over-riding physically will make a horse
tense and shorten his stride. It can make even a beautiful mover

look choppy. On the other hand, an ordinary mover can look beautiful under a relaxed, balanced, and compassionate ride. Paul was an example of a rider who worked too hard. He was a very determined and dedicated rider. Every time he rode, his determination and hard work produced sweat beyond belief. I saw Paul only occasionally because he lived far away, so before the lesson I rode Paul's horse to help me in diagnosing the problems. Paul's horse was dead to the leg and had a laid-back attitude. No wonder Paul had to work so hard. He pushed the horse physically rather than using his mind to find a solution. Paul was exhausted from his physical work; the horse was exhausted from Paul's nagging. I recognized the problem immediately and rode the horse for a few minutes with a light leg and the appropriate use of the whip. The problem was cured. Next month there was far less sweat.

Mental energy gives you the patience and creativity to be diplomatic in training your horse. You finesse, rather than fight the horse or allow him to fight you. Once diplomatic discipline is established, the horse will respect his rider and trust him. Only when he trusts his rider will he relax and move freely.

Whenever there is a confrontation, whether with a horse or with other people, the temptation is either to fight or to give in. Holding to your principles takes a lot of mental energy, but it always wins with your horse and usually wins in life. It is mental energy that keeps you from submitting to anger because you are being threatened, or from being too permissive because it is easier not to argue.

Your spiritual energy urges you to go beyond the mechanical aspects of working with your horse. It motivates you along your journey beyond the mirrors. While your mental energy encourages you to read and *think about* attitude, superiority, humility, relaxation and the other essentials for unity with your horse, it is your spiritual energy that *drives you to set goals and change* yourself where necessary. Your spiritual energy inspires your dreams about what you might become, by yourself or with your horse. It allows you to respect others for all they have to offer and it powers you to change even the most fundamental aspects of your being, if that change is necessary.

The result of using your spiritual energy is that you will give yourself up to your horse. You both will move with a greater amount of physical, mental and spiritual energy than either of you had alone. To see how this transformation works, watch a horse and rider that flow. Their harmony is the result of their combined and enhanced energies. The most impressive example I can remember was a musical freestyle dressage ride. The horse and rider glided across the ring in harmony with the music and with each other. Their harmony, as they danced together movement by movement, lifted themselves and the spectators almost to a state of ecstacy. Many of the spectators had tears in their eyes. You could feel the unity of their spirits as they joined together with the music.

Commitment

*Commitment to a goal helps you to go forward
in tough times because it is reason for not fleeing
or quitting. It does not produce
success, but it allows success to happen.*

*H*ave you ever had this experience? During a riding lesson
your instructor unexpectedly asks you to jump. You are
afraid, but you are unwilling to admit your fear. Pretending
not to be afraid, you try to follow your instructor's directions.
However, your uncertainty prevents you from committing to
the jump and the horse runs out (a disobedience usually caused
by lack of commitment). The instructor asks you to try again,
but again the horse runs out. Finally the instructor raises his
voice and frightens you more than the jump does. You head
for the jump again, this time committed as a result of the instructor's voice and persistence. All of these refusals could have

been prevented if you had been realistic about your abilities and shared your fear with your instructor or had allowed your commitment to overpower your fear.

Commitment also requires perseverance. Learning to do flying changes is a good example. Flying changes are difficult enough for the horse to learn and for the rider they can be one of the hardest lessons of all. Riders frequently spend months learning to do them correctly. I am reminded of Mary, a dressage rider who wanted to go to the top. She progressed very successfully through second level. When she tried to learn the flying change for her third level tests, her horse became nervous and anxious, as many do. Mary herself had a small problem with coordination and stiffness, but up to this point her successes had come relatively easily. After many months of practicing the flying change without mastering it, Mary became frustrated and began to question her own ability and that of her horse. Her instructor and her friends reminded her of the natural difficulty of this exercise, but it was Mary's commitment to her goal of riding at the *Grand Prix* level that got her through this tough period. Her commitment allowed her to spend another six months learning and perfecting the changes. The entire process took ten months but the results were very good. The necessary ingredients were patience, time, investigation and commitment.

Commitment can be self-imposed, as are most horse commitments. Horse commitments involve time, money, energy, love and the self-discipline to carry them out, but they can be terminated if necessary. Practicing these self-imposed commitments can strengthen the resolve to carry out even more important commitments imposed by society, such as marriage, parenting, school or jobs.

*Commitment to your horse assures that you
will give him your total attention, understanding,
care and love. Your commitment to your
horsemanship goal will be meaningless unless
it is accompanied by a commitment to your horse.*

When man domesticated the horse, he assumed the obligation to look after his needs. You must recognize that the horse requires more caring than the car parked in your garage and be committed to filling his personal needs. Give him good quality feed, feed him on schedule, provide regular medical treatment, care for his feet. A happy, relaxed, and contented horse is more willing to please, so if you find it difficult to meet the financial or scheduling obligations for your horse, how can you expect him to perform at his best.

It is easy to short-change a horse's schedule. Do you always feed on time in the morning? Or do you sleep in an extra hour after a late-night party? If you are a careful, caring owner you realize that that hour is more important to your horse than to you. Mentally, your horse may lose his ability to trust you. He counted on you to arrive at 6 AM to give him his long awaited breakfast. By 6:15 he is anxious. By 6:30 he is nervous or irritated. By 6:45 he is banging on his door, fighting with his neighbor or walking his stall. Once fed, a particularly high strung or nervous horse could colic or founder. The negative consequences of your lateness are the chance your horse has to hurt himself physically and the loss of trust in humans that may occur if he does not know when his natural needs for food and water will be met.

Discipline

*You must discipline yourself
before you can discipline your horse.*

T here are many aspects to self-discipline, but I find that many people never get past the first step. Self-discipline requires looking honestly into yourself. It is especially important when something does not work as expected. As you look inward, question "What did I do or fail to do that could have caused this problem?" If you know yourself, your goals and your horse, the answer will be a valuable tool to finding the solution. Looking inward as a first step is a very difficult discipline in itself. Human nature does not prepare you to look inward. Human nature allows you to find fault with something other than yourself.

One of my students was having difficulty learning the sitting trot. Just as she was getting the rhythm, but before it was confirmed, she became ill. She missed two weeks of riding and had to start over. Several weeks later and on the verge of a breakthrough, her car broke down. No transportation. Again she had to start over. After another week on the lunge line, she decided it was the horse's fault that she couldn't sit properly. She would not believe that it was her irregular riding and subsequent stiffness that were causing the problem. She tried another horse. No success. Four stables and nine months later, she still had not succeeded. Why? She never had the self-discipline to accept that the problem was her irregular riding. She did not believe she was stiff. She was unwilling to evaluate herself honestly, so her frustration outweighed her progress and she stopped riding.

Another student showed the positive effects of self-discipline. Lilly was riding at a high level, but she did not keep her leg on the horse. She tended to make horses nervous because of her dangling lower leg. She consented to be lunged with her stirrups tied to the girth until the problem was solved. Within a month she was off the lunge, her leg was correct and horses were no longer nervous with her. Why? She made no excuses. She accepted the responsibility for making horses nervous and dedicated herself to doing something about it.

In disciplining your horse, make a correction with whatever degree of force is required to make the message clear. Once the horse responds, immediately treat him with love as though there had never been resistance.

Your correction tells your horse you do not want him to behave a certain way. He changes. Your loving praise tells him he is now doing what you want. He learns more from the praise than from the punishment for now he knows how you want him to perform.

Many horses are lazy about answering the leg to go forward. I use my leg, followed by a snap of the whip. If no answer, I use the whip again, harder. The second he moves forward I reward him. I asked; he has learned. Now it is clear — a soft squeeze of the leg means move forward immediately. This is much better than constantly nagging, which usually results in a deadening of the aids.

Although a correction is a form of punishment, the subsequent reward allows trust to develop. The reward can be as subtle as a softening of the aids or a relaxing of the back. The horse relaxes and moves freely.

Discipline must be given carefully. You must always remember to love the animal; you must be diplomatic; you must never act in anger. Otherwise, it causes confusion, pain and fear worse than the original undesirable behavior, and the consequences take many hours of training to undo.

The negative consequences of poorly administered discipline can be seen in an example from the dressage ring. At "C" Bill's horse begins to question his pace at the trot. By "E" he is going quite fast. Not until "E", sixty feet after he began to speed up, does Bill use a half-halt. The horse wonders "What does the rider want? He is pushing and pulling like mad. What am I to do?" He goes a little slower, but not as slow as Bill had intended. Bill continues to hold. At "A" the horse decides to get crooked to see if that is what he wants. Bill still pushes and pulls. Now the horse is confused and his mouth and back hurt. He resists and locks his jaw. Finally Bill halts, totally frustrated with the horse. What happened? The first error was that he did not catch the problem when it began at "C". The second error was his failure to reward the horse for his initial response. If Bill had softened his aids and then given a second half-halt, instead of locking his seat and hands, the horse would have slowed and relaxed.

Bill could have made a different error with his discipline. He could have jerked the horse in the mouth the moment he began to speed up. This would have been too strong a reaction. The horse would say "Ouch! What does Bill want? That hurt my mouth!" Consequently, Bill's horse would put his head high in the air, tightening his back muscles, shortening his stride and losing rhythm. Now Bill really has a problem because the slightest squeeze of his fingers will cause the horse to resist further in his back and jaw. He has lost his horse's trust.

Why would a rider be late in responding or jerk his horse's mouth? Anger, carelessness, lack of rhythm, lack of confidence, lack of education are a few possible causes. A rider must include love, compassion and education with his discipline in order to respond correctly to the action of the horse. It takes mental, and perhaps spiritual, energy to learn to communicate appropriately with his horse.

Bill could have had discipline with compassion and love if he had understood some basics about the horse's mind: The horse needs **immediate** correction; he cannot remember at "E" what he did at "C." The horse has a low threshold for pain; a strong correction may produce fear. The horse needs **prompt** and **clear** praise; after a strong half halt, immediate softening of the aids is essential. Corrections, even late ones, made with compassion and loving discipline are acceptable if the horse feels the rider's love. The rider must first learn to discipline himself, to do things as correctly as possible and on time. Second, he must accept an error on his part. Third, he must believe that his horse wants to listen if the error is explained correctly. Fourth, the rider must have a clear idea of what he is attempting to do. Fifth, he must act immediately, responding to the horse with either an affirmation or a correction.

Patience

*Learn to do one thing at a time until
it becomes second nature.*

E veryone wants quick results. It is difficult to give patient
    time to horse, instructor and self. Yet maximum results
come from learning one thing at a time until it becomes part
of your basic nature. Each new skill must be confirmed in your
total being. This is true for your horse too. Confirmation takes
practice and time. To quote Henry Wynmalen's book *Dressage*,
"In riding, one principle must be mastered thoroughly before
the next one is attempted; in riding, it is thoroughness that
is quick and speed that is slow."

If you expect faster progress than you or your horse is
capable of, one or both of you will become frustrated. Frustration may produce fear, tension, confusion, inability to communicate, or lack of coordination between mind and body.

Behavior and confidence will deteriorate. A patient rider can avoid these negative reactions.

*Respond to mistakes or disobedience
without irritation, frustration, or loss of temper.*

Horses, like people, can have a bad day. When you are with your horse you must be able to put aside your complex, overly scheduled life and take each minute as it comes. Otherwise, if something goes wrong, you will find it difficult to keep control. You will fail to consider that your horse might simply be having a bad day. Loss of patience is negative and creates aggressive behavior with emotional involvement. The horse becomes fearful and loses any confidence and trust he may have had. Fear can undo months of training.

Suenig put the need for patience in the following way:

Anyone who loves his horse will be patient, and patience, inexhaustable patience — especially when psychological and physical defects are present — is necessary to make the horse understand what we want of it. Patience is equally necessary in order not to grow immoderately demanding, which always happens when we do not reward an initial compliance by immediate cessation of demand, but try to enjoy a victory until the horse becomes cross or confused.

At a show I watched with horror a horse's treatment as he left the ring after knocking down a rail. He was prepared for his mistreatment; he had been abused before. His tail got tighter and tighter until he held it rigidly between his legs; his ears went back; the whites of his eyes were showing. No wonder. The moment he was out of the ring, his rider began kicking and jerking his mouth. His bit was a twisted wire snaffle, so the pain aggravated his fear. To restore trust between rider and horse would take years of gentle handling. There is no justification for this kind of treatment. A horse's mind cannot associate a fence knocked down with punishment a few minutes later. He probably knocked the rail down because of his fear of leaving the ring, for the fence was the last one before the out gate. This was abuse, not correction, because it was too long in duration, came too long after the mistake and was too emotional.

Be patient with yourself and your own progress.

It is a big job for your body to coordinate your mind and spirit. You were not born on a horse. You do not instinctively communicate with your legs while your hands remain passive. Your natural movements must be tailored to coincide with the needs of your horse. You have much to learn about how to influence the horse tactfully and consistently and it is no easy job to put your mind into his. Acquiring the appropriate attitudes and goals for yourself and your horsemanship may take years of self-analysis and work. Sometimes it is difficult to accept the need for patience with our own being. In *Thoughts to Live By,* Maxwell Maltz suggests you approach your personal development slowly; "Don't make haste or make waste, but sit in the quiet room of your mind and use your imagination creatively to relax, to control your fears, anxieties and uncertainties, to find tranquility through patience."

Praise

Praise your horse, yourself, and others for jobs well done.
Praise removes the stress of uncertainty, promotes
self-esteem, and makes the recipient eager to repeat the job.
Praise must not give a false impression.

P raising your horse tells him when his behavior is acceptable. Punishing can only tell him what not to do. Praising your horse with a kind word, a softening aid, a pat or a carrot will give lasting results toward relaxation. When you stroke your horse with your hand have you ever felt him relax his body as though to say to you. "Thank you. You DO love and appreciate me"?

Acknowledging a horse through praise is one of the most valuable tools used in training. Praise makes the horse feel good, feel comforted, feel his efforts are appreciated. Why do animals react positively to praise? It is the confirmation of self-worth. Praise will build a closer relationship between you and your horse.

When you praise your horse, you must realize that you also did well. You are a team and his success is also yours. Acknowledging expected results aids growth by promoting relaxation, self-esteem and security. The stress of uncertainty is removed. Praise is an essential ingredient of success. When you experience honest praise, you feel good and you want to repeat the action. So does your horse.

Schooling your horse allows many, often overlooked, opportunities for praise. In riding a good corner, you bend your horse around your inside leg. If your horse goes deeply into the corner, he is responding to your aids. A wise rider will reward his horse in the corner by softening his aids. Both you and your horse will relax. The horse's physical relaxation will allow his muscles to build. His mental relaxation will increase his level of trust. You can test the success of your actions by a simple act: If the horse is correctly bending around the inside leg, you can pat him with your inside hand, allowing your inside rein to loop, and the horse will not lose his rhythm or his bend. You can then praise yourself for a well-done effort in communication.

Many people find it difficult to praise themselves. If you have this problem, you may be able to overcome it by first learning to praise your horse. It is easy to praise your horse. If you give him quality time and attention, his naturally cooperative attitude will offer you many opportunities to praise him.

Giving praise has been a difficult skill for me to learn. My theory was that if everything was good, I said nothing. Recently I realized how inadequate this theory was. I never slighted praising my horse because I understood that my horse needed constant reassurance. My attitude toward people was more complex: Since each of my students rode by choice and was not the subject of another being's wishes, I believed they did not need reassurance. I was wrong. Now that I praise my students, I find there are many benefits. The student relaxes when I praise him and often reaches forward to pat his horse. The rider passes on the approval he feels to his horse. The horse relaxes, both from the pat and from the loss of tension in the rider.

*Because praise is such a powerful motivator,
it must not be given at the wrong time.*

You are riding in your indoor arena during a snow storm.
A sheet of snow falls off the roof. As it passes the window your
horse spooks and leaps halfway across the arena. If you pat
him he will interpret the pat as a reward. He may soon learn
that nice things happen when he spooks. Your efforts to soothe
him have given a false impression. You would have been better to stop him firmly, but gently, and take him back to the
spot where he shied. Only when he quietly passes the spooky
window should you praise him.

Some professionals deliberately give a false impression to
gain students. The trainer may promise fast progress and wins
at big shows, but once the student comes with the trainer full
time the student is manipulated to suit the trainer's wants.
Andy rode a lovely, but poorly trained thoroughbred at local
shows and clinics. At one clinic, the instructor was full of praise
and promises that Andy and her horse could become *grand prix*
jumpers in six months. Andy was thrilled. She had always
wanted to jump the *grand prix* courses. Naturally she forgot
that she was only jumping 2'6'' at the time. The whole family
made sacrifices so that Andy could move her horse and train
with this famous person. A year later, with all her money
spent, Andy could jump only 3'6'' courses and not with the
greatest confidence. Why? Andy seldom rode; she cleaned
stalls and groomed horses instead. Since she had not achieved
the goal she was promised, she felt she was a failure. She never
realized that she had been misled by the false praise in the first
place.

Some people mislead themselves with their own false

praise. Their bragging is really a sign of insecurity. They feel they must tell the world to help themselves believe they are good. Examining themselves and looking for their real strengths will allow them to develop a sense of self-worth based on truth. Gradually they will find the praise they were looking for.

Praise must be based on honest strengths, not on false impressions. When you see someone full of self-praise, evaluate not their words but their actions and results. Likewise, when you are praised, accept the praise graciously but recognize truthfully whether or not it is appropriate under the circumstances. When you praise others, especially your horse, be sure they know it. Allow the gratification of making others happy to be your reward.

Forgiveness

You must be able to forgive yourself and others for unacceptable behavior, and then forget.

Y ou must be able to forgive yourself and others in order to free your mind of negative thoughts. If your horse challenges you with unacceptable behavior, you must correct him and immediately forgive him. If your instructor gives you wrong information you must accept his apology and forgive him. If you make a wrong decision, you must forgive yourself. Forgiveness allows you to forget. If you do something you cannot correct, you also must be able to forgive yourself and forget it. It is a waste of emotion and energy not to complete the cycle. Past errors, problems, injuries or negative expectations retained through lack of forgiveness take up space in your mind, use energy and limit the possibility for positive experiences.

The ability to forgive and forget allows you to wipe away

anger, irritation or negative expectations. Otherwise, the horse, who is a sensitive creature, will feel your stress and lose relaxation or begin to resist you. He will no longer be able to use his body fully. Your stress is immediately transferred through your body to your horse. As explained by Wynmalen: ''[The horse] also stiffens up under the influence of fear, premonition and nervous tension. Under such conditions he cannot relax and without relaxation our search for suppleness becomes a hopeless quest.''

Learn to live for today, keeping in mind your future goal. Do not worry about the consequences of any incomplete or negative past experience. Even a negative experience can lead to positive growth if you evaluate it and record the results positively in your brain. Remember, your horse lives for the moment. His mind is not cluttered with the past or the future.

Imagery

*Through imagery you can construct a mental picture
of all aspects of an activity, including sight, sound,
rhythm, feel or smell. The picture
becomes a standard helping you to learn or
against which you can measure your performance.*

While you are mastering mentally the rudiments of riding, you also need to develop the intuitive, feeling side of your horsemanship. You need all your senses to relate closely to your horse. You can sharpen your sensitivity through imagery. By concentrating very hard on your riding, you will be able to memorize the sight, sound, smell and feel of the experience. It will be like storing a super video tape in your mind. You will be able to compare the way your horse looks or feels at the moment with the sight or feel of him on the video tape in your mind. You will know instantly whether you are correct. Also, this super video tape in your unconscious can guide you in learning new movements that you have only watched others perform. It allows you to anticipate how the preparation and execution should feel, even though you have never done them before.

The type of imagery you use depends on your level of riding. Beginners study only individual elements like position or the gaits of the horse, whereas more advanced riders concentrate on putting all of the elements together. What you are able to absorb into your mental picture will change automatically as your riding skill improves.

I have found many good uses for imagery. While mounted, I am able to reproduce the image of my horse's movement - the elasticity and muscle flexions - that I mentally photographed while lunging him earlier. Likewise, when I observe an outstanding performance by a top horse and rider, I memorize it to use later when I am instructing. I can watch a rider with a strong position and store in my memory both the picture and the feel of that position. When mounted, I can reproduce the picture and the feel in my own body. Before I enter the arena for a dressage, jumping or equitation ride, I run through the ride in my mind as though I were in the class. Imagery allows me to practice the perfect ride without even moving. Finally, in my personal life, I use imagery to view myself as others would see me.

How do you train yourself to use imagery? Empty your mind. Remove all outside disturbances. Concentrate on the image you want to reproduce. Start with a small sequence. Every day, allow yourself five to fifteen minutes to concentrate on the image you have saved. It may take several weeks until you have mastered the technique. Once mastered you can use imagery anywhere, any time.

To help you learn imagery, or to practice your new skill, lunge your horse. Watch the freedom of his joints, the elasticity of his muscles, the length of his stride. Hold the picture in your mind. Imagine what it would feel like if you were as soft and elastic as your horse. When you mount, try to recall the mental picture and your imagings. You should be able to ride with more freedom and beauty.

As an instructor, observe the performances of people you respect. Mentally photograph their performance, paying particular attention to their overall freedom and harmony. Note areas where your students need to improve. When you instruct, bring forward this mental picture to serve as an animated teacher's guide to help you give your student the most complete and up-to-date knowledge.

If position is a weakness for you, watch a rider with a strong seat. Study the rider's position in relation to the horse, his balance, his body angles, his suppleness, and especially the relationship or "feel" between the horse and the rider. Compare how you feel on a horse with the picture you are viewing. Once mounted, recall the picture and try to make yourself look and feel like the rider you observed.

Imagery is beneficial to the riding student, especially to one who cannot have frequent lessons. New skills can be practiced in the mind between lessons, while waiting for friends or cleaning tack. The student can practice both the mechanics and the feel of what he learned, making his next lesson more fun and more productive. I once taught a college student who used imagery. She took fifteen minutes after each lesson to review the feel of her body, her horse and her aids when the movement was correct. Each night before she went to sleep she practiced the movements in her mind. She actually felt as though she were on her horse, while she was lying there in bed. Once she had mastered the technique, she learned a new lateral movement each week. The results were impressive; she was learning lateral movements faster than students who rode every day.

As a competitor, you can use imagery in two ways. First you can use it to practice your performance before entering the ring. Let us use a dressage ride as an example. Each horse has typical habits or evasions that usually get worse under the stress of competition. Prior to entering the arena, ride through the test in your mind. Concentrate, not on the things that could go wrong, but on how you are going to ride positively through movements that habitually cause problems. If your horse tends to lose balance in downward transitions, rehearse your preparatory half halts and concentrate on how you will keep your body soft and relaxed. When you enter the arena, you should be able to ride with more freedom, and your unconscious mind will guide you through the movements you practice.

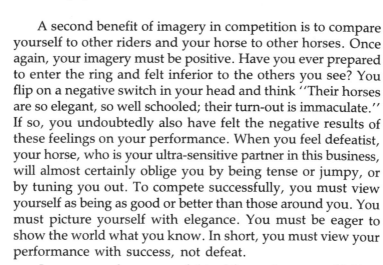

"Keep your self-image clean and bright. It is the window through which you see the world." (Maxwell Maltz)

A second benefit of imagery in competition is to compare yourself to other riders and your horse to other horses. Once again, your imagery must be positive. Have you ever prepared to enter the ring and felt inferior to the others you see? You flip on a negative switch in your head and think "Their horses are so elegant, so well schooled; their turn-out is immaculate." If so, you undoubtedly also have felt the negative results of these feelings on your performance. When you feel defeatist, your horse, who is your ultra-sensitive partner in this business, will almost certainly oblige you by being tense or jumpy, or by tuning you out. To compete successfully, you must view yourself as being as good or better than those around you. You must picture yourself with elegance. You must be eager to show the world what you know. In short, you must view your performance with success, not defeat.

Imagery can be a powerful tool for seeing yourself. Your understanding of information varies with the way you see yourself. Do you have a positive or negative attitude about yourself? For example, if you have big ears and you believe your ears are unacceptable, you will feel unattractive and think that everyone makes fun of your ears. If you feel this way you will promote your negative image in your communications.

Ask yourself the question: "Can I change my ears?" Of course the answer is "No." So, you must imagine that your ears are acceptable and come to accept them yourself. Practice regularly seeing yourself with acceptable ears. Look beyond your ears and find other parts of your body that you feel good about. As your view of yourself becomes more positive, your attitude toward life will change and your entire life will become more successful.

All communications are perceived as either positive or negative. If you feel you are unattractive, you will view all communications as negative. People do not view you negatively just because of your ears. But if you are self-conscious because of your big ears, you will give off negative vibrations that will be felt by others. Other people see the unattractive things about you only when you promote them. You probably promote your less attractive aspects unconsciously, but you do so whenever you have negative feelings about yourself. Remember that people look first for your good qualities.

Consider the implications of your self-image in relation to your horse. How do you want the judge to view you when you enter the show ring? If your self-image is positive you will feel better about yourself and have better relationships with people. Even your horse will respond. I have seen the effect of a positive self-image in my students who show. Those who enter the ring with self-confidence, head erect, sitting tall but relaxed, project confidence to their horse. They can perform successfully on almost any horse because the horse will move with the confidence he feels in his rider. Self-confidence, a by-product of a positive self-image, promotes better communication between horse and rider because the aids are clear and consistent. Both horse and rider emit positive vibrations which are easily recognized by a good judge.

Concentration

*Concentration is total attention to the subject at hand,
so that your body, mind and spirit are all
learning or acting simultaneously and in unison.*

T otal concentration allows quicker, more complete and more correct results. All parts of your being experience what you learn. Your muscles are learning new patterns of behavior, your brain is analyzing and storing what you learn, and the spiritual side of your nature is discovering a new way to relate to your horse, to others, or to the world.

When you are performing, total concentration allows you to ignore everything except what you are concentrating on. If you have pain you will not feel it; if it is raining you will not feel it; if a car horn honks outside the ring you will not hear it. All your muscles, sensory nerves, motor nerves and cognitive powers are focused on your horse and what you are doing. Both your conscious and unconscious minds are focused on the subject, so your actions are quicker, stronger and more accurate than you would normally expect.

How do you learn to concentrate? First, empty your mind of any preoccupations or unrelated thoughts. Second, breathe regularly and deeply. Third, focus on all facets of your present activity — sight, sound, feel, taste. Fourth, absorb everything you notice.

Your
"Mountain
Top"

When faced with important decisions, it is necessary to free your mind of clutter. Only with a tranquil mind can you sustain an adequate degree of introspection.

I magine yourself on a cold, crisp, winter morning riding your horse along a dirt road bordered by tall trees and a river. Snow is beginning to fall gently around you. Anyone would agree that this is a tranquil moment. The calmness and beauty of nature seem to take possession of you and your horse. The tranquility and serenity allow you to clear your mind and bring forward your deepest thoughts or to leave your mind empty and totally free to relax.

I call the external place where I find such tranquility my "mountain top." Everyone should have a "mountain top" somewhere. At times when you must make a major decision, you must be able to clear your mind and focus only on the subject of concern. On your "mountain top" you can analyze a problem, plan your goals, practice imagery, or evaluate your progress. It is an expansion of the techniques you learned in "On hold" and "Imagery," useful to foster introspection.

You may find your "mountain top" wherever you feel the most calm. It probably will be a place where you can be undisturbed. It may be a place you already know, where you go now to do your thinking. I find that my time alone in the stable feeding the horses is a time of deep thought. Another is when I stop to watch them grazing in the field. Still another is a quiet hack in the country. Sometimes just going to the stable at a particularly stressful moment and joining in spirit with a tranquil horse can help me to emtpy my mind and find my "mountain top." I find that horse lovers are one step ahead of other people in finding their "mountain top."

Empathy

*Empathy allows you to put yourself into the mind
of your horse or of another person to the point
where you can understand and accept
their motivations, attitudes and actions.*

A s a riding instructor and trainer of horses, I have long
used this tool to learn quickly why a rider is having trouble or a horse is resisting. If I can put myself in a horse's body
and mind I feel both the "what" and the "why" of the problem. When I understand the "why," I can solve the problem
permanently. Correcting only "what" the horse is doing is
superficial, like treating the symptoms of a person's illness
without getting at the cause.

As a rider, you can increase your appreciation of your horse
and his trust in you if you can see his performance from his
point of view. If he is stiff and unwilling to accept the bit, is

it because he is just having a bad day? Is it because his muscles are sore? Is it because of distractions outside the ring? Or is it because your hands and arms are tense and unyielding? Answering these questions requires you to analyze all of the possibilities and try to imagine how each possibility would cause him to behave. You might have to try several solutions until you find the right one, but as you get to know your horse better, your track record will improve. When your horse realizes you won't ask anything unreasonable of him, he will trust you more and be more willing to try to do what you ask.

Being able to put yourself in the body and mind of another person will improve the quality of your relationships. There will be greater understanding and acceptance of other problems and points of view. Your open mind will make you less judgmental and therefore kinder. You won't want to hurt someone if you can see yourself in their place. As you come to recognize their motivations and attitudes, you will develop a better appreciation for who they are. You will be able to enjoy them and learn from them even if there is little in common between you.

The
Journey
To
Beyond

Introduction

With the resources you have developed, you are ready to journey beyond the mirrors. Your goals may be clear, but the journey may not be easy or direct. This journey requires you to examine, evaluate and, perhaps, change your attitudes and aspirations both toward your horse and toward life. You may feel comfortable where you are, or afraid of the future, and not want to make the changes necessary to advance. Or, you may need to develop additional physical or mental resources necessary for the next step in your spiritual growth. Do not try to take shortcuts, because failure to adequately develop a skill or evaluate and change an attitude could jeopardize your journey. Take one step at a time and gradually you will move yourself toward inner-harmony, your horse toward maximizing his natural beauty, and the two of you toward a unity of your spirits.

Attitude

Your attitude is your point of view toward yourself,
your horse and the world. Your attitude determines
whether you can learn and grow from your experiences.
Having a positive attitude toward life
is a necessary first step along your journey.

*I*n many ways this entire book is about your attitude toward
life. I started with a premise that you, as a reader, want to
improve your horsemanship and your own personal relationship to life. That is, I assumed that you would have an open,
receptive and responsive attitude toward learning, and that
you would be willing to examine yourself honestly and change
yourself where necessary. My assumption is that you are
basically open-minded, eager to learn about horses and
yourself, and willing to try a new approach once its value has
been made clear to you.

Attitude

Positive attitudes are important. On a bright, sunny morning everything seems right with the world. You are happy to be alive, laugh when you see that your horse spilled his water bucket all over the stall the night before, and don't even mind fixing the fence where the pony broke through to get the fresh, spring lawn grass yesterday. You enjoy your horse's over-eager gait and humpy back when you go for a ride. A week later, you wake up grumpy and groggy from a poor night's sleep. Your horse kicks at his door in anticipation of breakfast and you yell at him. The stalls are a mess and you think you will never get through cleaning them. When you ride, your horse moves crookedly, won't halt squarely, and tosses his head when you try to put him on the bit. You swear that you're going to sell him and buy a "decent" horse. These day-to-day changes in attitude affect everybody and are relatively minor, but they demonstrate how critical a positive attitude can be to your horsemanship. Joe Hyams in *Zen in the Martial Arts* expresses the idea metaphorically:

> The mind is like a fertile garden...It will grow anything you wish to plant — beautiful flowers or weeds. And so it is with successful, healthy thoughts or negative ones that will, like weeds, strangle and crowd the others. Do not allow negative thoughts to enter your mind for they are the weeds that strangle confidence.

A person is not born with a certain set of attitudes. Not only does your approach to life change daily, depending on how you feel, but also you can change it at will. Examine your attitude about yourself. Accept what you cannot change and change what is changeable. First, engage in honest self-examination and rejoice in the positive. Accept anything you have no control over — like feelings of shame, embarrassment or fear. Change what you can — like your willingness to try new ideas, or the feeling that you always must be in charge. Maxwell Maltz said: "If you look for the good, you will learn to overlook evil." Everyone has some degree of insecurity, inhibition, shyness or confusion. Your ability to resolve these conflicts and see the good aspects of your life will determine the degree of success you have with your horse and your life.

Although you cannot avoid all conflicts, you can work through them, allowing yourself to put aside the negative feelings and attitudes they generate so you can proceed positively with your horse and your life. I never want to hurt anyone and consequently I dread having to fire an employe. One day I tried to school a young horse, knowing that after I rode I would have to fire my working student. I had problems I had never had before with that horse. I walked and thought about the situation. I realized that my concern over hurting this girl was affecting me more deeply than I could control. I got off the horse, fired the girl, and got back on. I went for a short hack to clear my mind and calm my emotions, and then continued training. It was one of the best sessions I had ever had. I learned several important lessons. I still hate to fire people, but I learned to be honest with myself, not to avoid what I dread, but to do it and forget about it. The lesson demonstrated how important a positive attitude is to horsemanship. Nothing of value can be accomplished with the horse if the rider's mind is filled with negative attitudes.

There are several attitudes helpful to both horsemanship and life. Your desire to learn must be an open-ended, inner commitment, allowing you to evaluate all new information. There is an endless stream of new material, techniques, approaches, so you must be committed to learning throughout your entire life.

You should have the attitude that it is your responsibility to understand your horse, not that it is his responsibility to understand you. Your horse naturally wants to respond to your requests if they are communicated accurately. Your accuracy varies with how well you understand your horse. If you succeed, he will trust you. Assuming the responsibility for accuracy also works well in human communications. How many arguments ensue because neither person wants to take the blame for misunderstanding the other one?

When you work with your horse, you ask him to submit to your intentions. His natural reaction is to try to please you. Your attitude must reflect loving superiority, not forceful control. His attitude will be one of acceptance, not fear.

An example of a harmful attitude is one where you anticipate failure. If you think either you or your horse will be unable to perform a new task, probably you will be unable to do it.

As an instructor, I frequently see the results of a negative attitude. Whether it is at a cross country fence or an umbrella for the dressage judge at "C", the rider who has a negative attitude usually will have a disobedience. Likewise, a competitor rides either better or worse in the ring, depending on his attitude about himself and showing. Often I have enjoyed the beauty of a horse's movement in the warm-up. When he enters the ring the movement changes, the gaits become restricted, the rhythm becomes inconsistent, the jaw tenses. Much of this is because the rider is expecting problems in the ring.

If you see things with a positive attitude, you can find a solution. For example, Maxine's horse does not want to take the left lead. I think the problem is caused by lack of straightness, but Maxine is not quick enough with her communications to correct the problem. I ride the horse. As I straighten him and ask for the left lead, I explain to Maxine what I am doing. When the horse understands and takes the left lead consistently, Maxine remounts. Now she can experience the correct feeling. Maxine has three choices: First, she could feel good because she saw that the horse was capable of doing what was asked of him. Second, she could feel inferior because she could not do it herself. Third, she could refuse to believe that the problem was really hers. If she makes the second choice, her feelings of inferiority will prevent her from absorbing everything she saw, heard and felt about her horse. If she makes the third choice, she will not change her communications and the horse will revert to his old habits. Only if she makes the first choice will Maxine's confidence improve and will she be able to maintain what she and the horse learned.

Maintaining positive attitudes requires constant surveillance. It is very easy to slip into old habits.

Decision-Making

To progress personally or in horsemanship you must be confident of your ability to make dependable decisions.

P eople often avoid making a decision because they are afraid of making a mistake. How often have you stood motionless while something bad happened, thinking "What should I do? What should I do?" You probably know very well what you should do, but your conscious mind is very busy trying to sort out all the benefits and detriments of each alternative. You want to be "right." You don't want to worry about whether or not you made the correct decision, but instead you may feel badly because you did nothing at all. People learn a variety of ways to avoid decisions, often because they are afraid. Avoiding decisions leaves an unresolved cycle of communication in your mind. The void is filled by a sense of inadequacy leading to unhappiness, confusion, depression, alcoholism, drug abuse or illness.

Indecision means that you recognize a problem, but you do not know how to handle it or what to decide. With indecision, you know there is a need for action, but there is no emergency and you have time to get more information so you can make the right decision. If you have a problem while riding, but you do not know what to do, stop until you can get more information. In this case, indecision is a smart decision. For example, Tim is lunging a horse that does not want to be lunged. The horse pops his shoulder and pulls away from Tim toward the barn. Tim tries yelling, beating on the ground and sitting on the lunge line, but none of these methods works. Finally, Tim asks for help and learns how to control the horse. Either Tim or the horse could have been hurt if Tim had decided to persevere on his own.

Lack of confidence may also create indecision. Once you learn something you must discipline yourself to use the knowledge. It is through use that knowledge becomes confirmed, you gain confidence and you can use what you learned.

Indifference is another way to avoid making decisions. Indifference means that you do not care enough to muster the mental energy necessary to make a decision. There is no room for indifference in a horseman's life. Why be involved in such a complex sport if you are indifferent? If you do not care, you fail to observe important changes in your horse's habits. Unintentionally, you can train him to be an outlaw, as Kim did with her horse Spot. Kim rode Spot in combined training events, but she was really more interested in her social life. She treated Spot like a person, always giving him treats and thinking it cute when he nipped her hand or pocket. Soon he became a serious biter. Shortly after Kim sold Spot, he bit his new owner's hand seriously enough that she had to go to the hospital. Kim was shocked. She had avoided deciding what to do about Spot's biting by being indifferent to its danger and thinking it cute.

At times it is imperative that you make a decision right away. If your horse is disobedient or badly frightened, your survival may depend on your ability to decide correctly, immediately. Perhaps your horse whirls and bolts when he sees a big sheet of plastic blowing in the wind. Your unconscious mind stores knowledge and skills for times like these when you need to make a reactive decision. Your body responds to the emergency, staying on the horse and gradually stopping him without frightening him further — all without your conscious review of what to do.

Riders frequently make decisions based on inadequate knowledge of themselves or their horses. They try to ride horses that are too much for them or perform activities that are too difficult. Because the initial decision was wrong they get themselves into situations where no amount of split-second decision making ability can save them because they do not have the physical or mental tools to work with. A rider may know what to do but be physically unable to carry it out because of the size, strength or speed of the horse, or because of his own poor balance or seat. During a jumping lesson, Mary's horse bucked right after the fence and Mary did not have good enough balance to stay on. She somersaulted and landed directly under the horse's galloping hooves. Only because her horse made a super effort to miss her did she avoid having her chest crushed. A rider also may be unable to make a good decision because he does not have enough information about the options, understand what the problem is or know the proper aids. Sue's horse became excited when it saw other horses jumping. In trying to control her horse, Sue pulled back on the reins so much the horse became frightened, reared and ran off. Sue could not stop her horse and she did not know that she was safer on top of him. She bailed out and was badly hurt.

Avoiding potentially dangerous situations is a reason to have the advice of a good instructor and to follow the advice. The instructor will try to match your riding activity to your knowledge and skill level and will insist you practice new skills until they become second nature. Only when your knowledge and riding skills are a part of your total being can your decision-making ability be truly effective.

Where do you draw a line between being so cautious that your horsemanship never advances and so rash that you are constantly overfacing yourself? The choice of how fast to proceed requires careful evaluation by rider and instructor. To progress with your horse you must make decisions every day. Gradually, you learn to accept responsibility for your decisions, even if, at first, the responsibility is painful. Indecision about your abilities or with your horse would produce no results. Incorrect decisions would lead to results other than what you expected. You can ask your horse again, in another way. Your horse will immediately respond to your new request unless you have created fear or confusion for too long a period of time. If either you or your horse become fearful, confused or angry, the best decision may be to ask for something small that you can do easily and then seek assistance from your instructor. In time you will learn what is correct because you will get the anticipated result. The confidence gained by making small decisions daily with your horse will carry over into all aspects of your life.

Awareness

Awareness takes you beyond the mechanics of your riding.

O n the one hand, your awareness is the breadth or scope of your senses, as in how alert you are to what is going on around you. In this sense, your awareness can be likened to your antennae. Sally Swift would say you had "soft eyes." You realize that someone is standing behind you even though the person is out of sight and has made no noise. This form of awareness is, I think, a function of the unconscious mind. Even though the recognition of the "presence" is conscious, its existence is absorbed into your mind without active mental involvement. It allows you to absorb the feel of how to perform a new motor skill through passive observation, rather than through verbal instruction. A good example is the way teenagers learn to dance. They do not learn steps and patterns; they feel the music and the steps and patterns come spontaneously. Otherwise, they would be stiff as a board. They watch their friends; they listen to the music; and they dance! On the other hand, your awareness also refers to the sharpness of your senses, as in your ability to focus your attention. I think this form of awareness is a function of the conscious mind where you deliberately examine every aspect of your activity to discover its strengths and weaknesses, how it does and should feel. It is an analytical way of learning even though it, too, is based on observation. Watch a rider learning her diagonals. By focusing all her attention on the feel of the horse's movement in relation to her body when she is on the left or right diagonal, she memorizes how to differentiate the feel. She may not be able to select the correct diagonal automatically as she trots to the right or the left, but she can tell which diagonal she is on without looking down. She is conscious of where her body is in relation to the horse's legs.

Natural awareness, either broad or focused, varies greatly among individuals. We are not as clever as our horses at using our unconscious mind to sense attitudes or feelings. Someone hiding his real personality behind a screen can often fool us, whereas our horse recognizes that person's real nature. I once hired a stable manager who had good references and seemed acceptable to me. As with all new help, she came on trial. First, I began to notice that many of the horses put their ears back when she entered the stall. In a few days they became nasty. She reported to me that she had been kicked and bitten. When I asked her specifically which horses were the trouble makers, I was shocked: they were not our ornery horses. From the horses' reactions I realized she did not love horses. I did not keep her. Her character was not acceptable, but the horses with their greater ability to sense true feelings were first to be aware of it.

How can you expand your awareness? Look for barriers you may have erected to block your sensitivity. Either your broad or your focused awareness may be limited if you are under stress from your job, your health, your family, or are otherwise preoccupied. You may find yourself forgetting what you came to the store to buy, or turning the wrong way when you come out of your lane. You are not living in the present place and time, but in an inner world of your worries. Your mind is closed to the subtleties of human or horse relationships. Professional help to solve the problem or to teach you how to cope with the stress can make it possible for you to find greater awareness.

Meditation, yoga, TM and prayer are ways to increase awareness. They teach you techniques for clearing your mind, recognizing what you are really doing and why, understanding how your body feels under various conditions and how to change it. You learn how to empty your mind of all extraneous thoughts so you can feel more at one with everyone and everything around you. You learn not to try so hard so that your body can operate at its full effectiveness without mental interference. The same techniques work to make you aware of everything that is going on with your horse. You are quicker to sense his response to your aids, so you can either change the aids or reward him immediately. He becomes happier and more willing to work for you.

A specific way to increase your focused awareness and learn a great deal about your horse is to learn to massage him. You learn where he likes to be rubbed, how fast and how hard. No amount of reading can teach you how to massage. It is a feel you acquire with every horse you do. Since the massage is so personalized, you have to concentrate to identify the feedback from each horse. This practice will gradually make you more aware with all your horse activities.

Expectations

Your expectations provide steps along the way
toward your goal. Meeting them
should be a realistic measure of your progress.

Your expectations must be clear and realistic, yet flexible. Your horse never thinks back over what might have been, but you do. If your expectations are too high, you will feel disappointment and frustration. If too low, you may put in a mediocre performance because you are not asking enough of yourself. You must know yourself and your horse and be open to adjusting for unexpected circumstances if you are to develop appropriate expectations. Your ability to balance your hopes and your expectations is necessary to achieve inner-harmony.

It is important that the rider establish his own expectations. You may not even be aware of their influence, but family and friends can lead you to set unrealistic expectations. Because

Aunt Millie is bringing all your cousins to the next horse show, you convince yourself that you are ready to ride in some more difficult classes. If you were honest with yourself you would realize that you are not ready to jump 3' courses. You tell Aunt Millie that you "expect" to be ready. You aren't, and your rounds are poor. Your discouragement sets your riding back by several weeks.

Instructors often influence their pupil's expectations. The instructor suggests you enter your horse in a First Level dressage test. Because you like your instructor, you assume you must be ready for first level. You expect success. In a situation like this, it is important to know your instructor's intention. Perhaps she feels it is necessary for you to have the experience. You must set your own expectations about the ride based on what you know of yourself and your horse and how you have performed in your schooling sessions.

Many considerations go into selecting the right expectations. Anna was fully employed, a parent, and involved in the community. She had been riding for two years and decided she wanted to show. She expected the same success in showing that she had had in her past activities. Trouble errupted when her horse proved more complex than her tennis racket! Her show season did not meet her expectations. Anna re-evaluated herself, her riding and her other activities. She loved horses and wanted to continue riding, but she decided her schedule was not sufficiently flexible for her to meet the demands of showing. She concentrated on fox hunting and found it far more pleasurable.

Sarah is an example of someone whose expectations gradually moved her toward a long-term goal. Sarah's goal was to win the Medal finals. Every day she rode, she worked toward this goal. She had a progressive training plan that included expectations of daily progress and wins at certain shows. Her expectations were well thought out and realistic. She had a much better chance of satisfying her expectations and meeting her long-term goal.

Having short-term expectations about performance is also extremely important in horsemanship. They are one of the basis of communication between you and your horse. Remember Bill, whose horse wouldn't slow his trot in a dressage test? When Bill finally gave the aids for a half halt to slow his horse's trot, he wasn't clear in his own mind what to expect. The horse did slow down, but not as much as Bill thought was necessary. Bill's legs and hands remained clenched and the horse became confused. Bill expected too much change in speed all at once. His expectations were not realistic. Also, Bill was wrong in not recognizing his horse's small response. Because he was looking for too much, Bill did not reward what he got. His expectation was a giant leap rather than a small step toward his goal.

Confrontation

Problems become worse if ignored.
They don't stay the same or get better.

A s Robert Schuller says in *Tough Times Never Last, But Tough People Do!*, "The one battle most people lose is the battle over fear of failure... try... start... begin... and you'll be assured you won the first round."

Emotional strength is necessary to confront a problem, to manage a disagreement, or cope with a failure. Confrontation is vital for emotional stability. At first notice of a problem, you should define it, consider it, seek to correct any miscommunications, and then act and trust the results. Failure to confront the problem will result in coloring your attitude and cluttering your mind.

Lynn represents the proper way to confront a problem in horsemanship. Her horse Blacky runs out the gate when she is riding and Lynn decides that Blacky simply wants to return to the stable. The next time he tries to run out the gate, Lynn is ready with the appropriate aids. Blacky does not understand that he must stay in the ring because earlier he was successful in running out the gate. Why not again? Lynn is firm, but she does not get rough. Blacky fights, but Lynn does not allow him through the gate and she wins. The next time around Lynn remains alert, but trusts Blacky and praises him with a soft pat. By confronting the problem without anger and hostility, and by following her correction with trust, Lynn preserved movement, relaxation and a trusting horse. Had she ignored the problem, Blacky would have continued to go out the gate and eventually Lynn would have had an even greater difficulty.

Humble
Superiority

Mentally you are superior to the horse,
but that does not give you the right to domineer over him.
Soften your control with humility
so you can allow the horse to be himself.

Man's mind is more intelligent than the horse's, and with this intelligence he should learn how to deal with the horse on the horse's terms. Man's mental and spiritual capacity obligate him to understand and respect the horse for what he is and what he has to offer, namely a tremendous potential for cooperation and physical beauty. Developing his understanding and respect actually puts man in a position of humility relative to the horse. Man recognizes those ways in which the horse's body, mind and spirit are superior to man's and he learns from the horse, preserving the horse's superiority and uniqueness even while training the horse to perform as he wishes.

To develop this attitude, you must first understand

yourself and your own place in the scheme of nature. I do not believe that man was placed on earth to manipulate the earth and its creatures exclusively to his own advantage. Rather, he was intended to live in harmony with nature. I agree with Willa Cather's statement about the Indians: "The land and all that it bore they treated with consideration; not attempting to improve it, they never desecrated it." If you are seeking harmony with your horse in your riding, you must accept this belief at least to some extent. Harmony, by definition, requires that the horse be allowed to be himself in equal measure to which you are yourself. You cannot be in harmony with a creature which you have dominated and subdued.

The implication to your horsemanship is that you must do what is appropriate for the horse. As the smarter, but weaker partner, it is appropriate that you be in control. You cannot allow disobedience or the horse will soon come to take advantage of you.

Suenig says we must learn:

> to use diplomacy instead of struggle in reaching our goal, but we should never avoid a struggle if the horse should notice that we were yielding. At such moment, yielding just once for the sake of not disturbing a good relationship at any price and maintaining friendship would be quite wrong, for this friendship loses its value if it is not based on respect, upon the animal's acknowledgement of man's superiority.

Sandy and her horse Beehive are an example of humble superiority at work. The only time Sandy could ride was feeding time and Beehive showed his irritation by laying his ears back and kicking while being girthed up. Beehive was an event horse whose aggressive attitude was helpful to his eventing success. But today he was genuinely crabby. Sandy recognized the reason for his bad attitude and took her time warming up. She did not let herself become angry or impatient when he resisted the aids, but rather spent extra time on suppling exercises and getting him to pay attention. The warm-up took twenty minutes instead of the normal ten, but finally

Beehive relaxed and they had a good school. If Sandy had been demanding, rough or impatient there would have been a battle of the wills and the session would have lasted for hours. But by recognizing Beehive's crabbiness as a natural response to being taken away from his food, Sandy was able to gain control over him quietly and diplomatically.

Today's society admires independence and control, and you probably learned at an early age to want to be in control. Good horsemanship requires you to learn to control your horse passively, relinquishing yourself for the sake of establishing unity with your horse. You remain in control of your horse, but you give up your controlling attitude and act with humility. In this way you actually gain more independence and control over both yourself and your horse. Because you love your horse, you do not demand; you ask, and your horse, which is an agreeable creature, quickly does all that you request.

Spiritual unity with your horse allows you to melt into him, understanding him and trusting him because you are so familiar with all his actions and behaviors. As you develop this bond of understanding, you will find yourself unable to dominate in an unkind or unloving way. For you the horse will make the extra effort and his image in the mirror will display his natural beauty. Beyond that image you will know you have achieved spiritual harmony.

Communication

The communication cycle must be clear and complete:
question, answer, acknowledgement.

Communication requires that you understand yourself and know exactly what you want. Clarity about what you want enables you to communicate effectively and offer something of value. How do you develop clarity? You must know yourself and you must know your horse. When questions arise, you must proceed only when you have full understanding of the mission or direction. To fully understand, you must feel free to question your instructor or yourself. Once you understand, you must try to follow your understanding in your actions.

Your instructor gives you one explanation and expects you to do the shoulder-in. You try, but you do not succeed. Why? Do you understand the directions? Is your body cooperating with your mind? Do you know what a shoulder-in feels like?

Do you feel ready? Does your horse understand the aids? You must ask yourself these questions very quickly. The answers will tell you how to proceed.

For any new movement, you must first be sure you understand the movement. Exactly how much bend should you expect in the beginning. How do the hind feet track in relation to the front feet? Which rein do you use to move the horse's shoulder off the track and keep it there? What do you do with the other rein? Finally you must clearly communicate all this to your horse. How much inside leg will he need to keep him moving along the wall instead of into a circle? Your horse will respond correctly as soon as he understands what you are asking. The key is to be sure you understand what and how you are going to ask the horse to do it.

It should be easy to communicate with your horse. Unless you have deadened him to your aids, he is always listening. Although he might be distracted by a dog leaping into the ring carrying a big stick, his attention is not divided between his lesson and what to cook for dinner or between his lesson and why his teenage son just ran away from home. He lives strictly in the present. Often the horse learns a movement more quickly than the rider.

You, too, must be able to clear your mind so that your tools of communication are completely available to you. You need to be alert, quick and responsive. You must be aware of when to be passive and when to be aggressive. Your communication may seem appropriate, clear and timely to you but not be at all so to your horse. You must try to put yourself in your horse's place. For example, your horse bites at you and you punch him in the nose. Your response was clear and timely, but maybe not appropriate. You had just patted him hard (a kind gesture, you thought) on the top of his neck where his muscles were sore after an hour of collected work. No wonder he bit at you! Think again about the half halt. If you acknowledge too soon you can make your horse nervous; if you acknowledge too late you can make him tense and resistant.

I learned these principles of communication by working with my horses. Eventually I found that they are equally valid for human communications. You should assume you are responsible for the clarity of your communications. To avoid feeling guilty because of a breakdown, you follow several steps to make your communications clear and complete: You ask a question, you listen to the answer, you acknowledge the answer. If the answer does not feel right, figure out why, and ask another question. I try never to leave a horse or a person with a bad feeling following a communication. If my feelings reveal awkwardness or discomfort, I find out why and remedy the situation immediately. Then I must accept the outcome.

*All communications should be positive,
never designed to hurt another being.*

All communications, both verbal and non-verbal, must be given with love and good intentions. The response will be positive, whether from horse or man. A communication made out of anger will provoke an unnecessary confrontation. Even if the words are polite, the listener will recognize the hostility and react to the feeling behind the words. While the positive communication promotes cooperation and good will, the hostile communication promotes discord and unhappiness, which are detrimental to inner-harmony.

Responsibility

As a horse owner you are responsible for your horse's
physical, mental, and spiritual well-being.
If you wish to share in the joys of success in life or
with your horse, you must accept the obligations.

A relationship with a horse is a relationship you enter
into voluntarily and when you do so you must be willing to accept the responsibility. Humans have domesticated
the horse, removing him from his natural environment, and
asking him to live under confining conditions. The horse is no
longer able to take care of himself because of the limits humans
have placed on his life. Now he is totally dependent on you
for food, shelter and all of his basic needs. Although you can
hire someone to feed and water him or to train him, you retain the responsibility for his care.

You also have the responsibility to solve any problems that
arise. No association with an animal or with another human

being is trouble-free. If you want to take pleasure in the good moments, you must take responsibility for the bad ones and for their correction. Problems get worse if they are ignored; they don't go away.

Your basic responsibility to your horse is to keep him in good physical, mental, and spiritual condition. You realize that you must look after his needs for food and water and exercise, but you also must learn to look after his unique needs. For example, some horses become bored easily when confined to their stalls; give them toys. Some horses are nervous when vanned; give them extra room. Some horses love water; give them an opportunity to swim.

I once bought an eight-year-old thoroughbred named Tex. He had spent the entire eight years of his life in a two acre pasture with his mother. When he was a three-year old, his teenage owner had been killed in an auto accident. The bereaved family was unable to deal with the emotional trauma of selling their daughter's horse. For five years, Tex had only his mother, a little feed, and some carrots. Loading Tex took eight hours, unloading him took three, and getting him through our stable door took another two. Tex had a good temperament, but every experience was new. With special attention to his insecurities, Tex developed into a normal competitive horse. During his first event, Tex and his rider turned too fast on slippery ground and fell on the cross country course. Before anyone knew they had fallen, Tex had galloped straight back to the van and was waiting to be loaded into his favorite stall. Quite an achievement for a horse who had recently taken eight hours to load!

It is your responsibility to understand your horse. It is you who are communicating your wishes to your horse. You must listen to his feelings by watching his ears and tail, looking into his eyes, and noticing any abnormalities in behavior. You must respond to him with understanding. If your horse seems resistant to what you had planned, do not force the issue. Rather, discover the cause of the problem and work through it as necessary. Create a new plan to solve whatever problem you discover.

Just as you are always careful to give clear communications to your horse, you must be equally careful to have clear expectations of the response. You must know what the correct response will feel like when it occurs, so that you can reward the horse clearly and promptly. The half halt is a good example because it is so frequently used and misused. The rider's job is to give the aid, recognize the result and go forward. If the response is unacceptable you must question yourself. Was the aid too late, out of sequence, too severe, or even just wrong. You must quickly review your actions, based on the premise that your horse's nature is to please. On the other hand, if your horse responds correctly to a half halt, you must reward immediately with a release. When it appears that the horse is not listening, it is usually because you were inaccurate or unclear. The horse rarely acts out of deliberate disobedience. On the other hand, there are many ways the rider could have acted irresponsibly, such as failure to reward, failure to recognize a response, failure to correct miscommunications, or failure to have clear expectations.

You are responsible for your own accomplishments.

Your first obligation is always to seek the truth. When there is a problem, you must be honest about its cause. Many people admit verbally that they have caused a problem, but they do not really believe it. Their admission is in words alone. The truth for you is what you believe in yourself, not what you say about yourself. If you say one thing and believe another, you cause conflict within yourself. If you do this with your horse he will be completely confused about your intentions.

Sam approaches a jump that he has reason to fear. His legs and voice tell Leo to jump, but in his heart he is sure Leo will stop. Leo feels Sam's legs banging, his voice clucking, but his body vibrations sucking back. Leo wonders what he is supposed to do, but he is a courageous, generous and well-trained horse, so he jumps. Sam's body never really intended to jump, so he is badly left behind. Sam reapproaches the jump, really frightened this time because he almost fell off. Leo's attitude is complicated by the pain in his back and he stops. This time Sam does fall off. Now Sam has an honest fear. If he can admit his fear, he can have the jump lowered and gradually regain his confidence. If he denies his fear he will also give his horse reason to fear jumping.

You may believe that dedication to the truth can cause you embarrassment. Like Sam, you may be reluctant to let others know you are afraid of jumping, so you deny it. But in reality, admission of the truth opens the door to solutions. The initial pain of embarrassment is replaced by confidence as you solve the problem.

Your pursuit of the truth requires you to be accurate. Your instructor may offer suggestions as to the cause of a problem, but only you can identify the real cause.

Susie was plagued with embarrassing performances in the dressage ring. Susie said it was her horse's nerves. I believed it was Susie's nerves. I thought her mind froze when she entered the ring, closing off her communication with her horse. When we discussed stress, Susie denied she felt any stress. She was being honest with me. She was unaware of any stress. Years later, Susie recognized and admitted to me that the dressage ring had caused her stress. Then she began to understand the performance problems. She no longer blamed her horse. She developed a program of stress reduction and her performance in the dressage ring improved dramatically.

Your responsibility for your actions extends to seeking help when needed. If you have used all your knowledge and skill to solve a problem and have failed, it is your responsibility to learn more. It is logical and important to go to an expert you trust. If you decide the recommendations make sense, you must try them with confidence.

A very attractive horse I was training had frequent problems in the show ring. He behaved inconsistently. I consulted several veterinarians and finally found the horse had a hormone imbalance. I never could have discovered the cause of the problem myself. The imbalance was corrected and gradually the performance problems disappeared.

It is also important to be sure that you really understand any advice or instruction you receive. You are denying responsibility for your actions if you pretend to understand or pretend to agree when you really do not. You will neither solve your problem nor progress if you deceive yourself. I see this schooling my students. They often ride round and round the ring saying they understand my corrections, but they never get any better because they do not accept the responsibility for understanding. They confine their learning to doing what I tell them only!

Owning success is equally important. Often people do not admit success out of a lack of confidence or out of a false modesty. But if you cannot accept success, how can you tell your horse when he is correct? It is important to acknowledge your horse's response immediately. You must be as quick to reward obedience as you are to correct mistakes. Therefore, you must look for success as well as failure. Its acknowledgement is important for the mental and spiritual well-being of both you and your horse.

I once had a rider, Lilly, who refused to admit success. Lilly had a lovely horse who was eager to please. But Lilly could never accept that something was good, so she never rewarded her horse. Her horse soon became crabby because he never knew when he was correct. Lilly's negative attitude eventually caused her horse's forward, alert ears to rotate backwards, exhibiting his confused unhappiness. Eventually Lilly gave up her horse. It is interesting to note that Lilly's sullen, unhappy attitude pervaded her entire life. The horse went on to a new owner and soon returned to being his eager, cheerful self, but Lilly never learned to accept her successes.

Relaxation

Relaxation is necessary for the rider to attain inner-harmony and for the horse to display his natural beauty.

R elaxation is a broad term that is often used loosely. Yet, the ability to relax is so critical to good horsemanship that the concept must be explored in all its ramifications. Relaxation must exist on three levels: Physical (suppleness), mental (clarity of mind and emotion) and spiritual (freedom from fear, anger, resentment, jealousy and other negative attitudes). Relaxation on all levels, resulting in unimpeded awareness, is the basis for spiritual growth that leads to maximum physical and mental performance and to inner-harmony.

Stresses affecting the mind or spirit often are manifest as physical tension. This is more true for people than for horses. The complexity of our minds and the interaction of our environment, culture, responsibilities and relationships exacerbate our stresses. On the other hand, our superior minds allow us to enjoy the simple things of life, as a horse would, even while we function as productive human beings. Observe your horse and let him teach you how to enjoy the basic things of nature.

The first step toward relaxation is learning to recognize and deal with the obstacles in your way.

Stiffness in either horse or rider is easily recognized and frequently addressed in books on horsemanship or training. To evaluate the horse for physical stiffness, watch him move freely in the pasture. Without the restrictions of a rider he will reveal his natural gaits and suppleness. Likewise, observe the rider while he is carrying on his normal daily functions, walking or running. A routine of simple exercises will alleviate natural stiffness in either horse or rider.

Tiredness or a recent injury may cause stiffness. Nina had been on a week-long ski holiday. She came home stiff and sore but at once went riding and tried to school her horse in his second level dressage movements. Her normally elastic muscles were stiff and tight; her aids became abrupt. Her lower leg usually followed her horse's rhythm as she asked him to move laterally but today it locked on his side causing him to scoot across the ring. Her tired arms pulled on the reins and her horse came above the bit and fought. It was obvious that Nina's tiredness had totally blurred her communications. For Nina the solution would be simple: either rest or take her horse on a quiet hack. She simply had to realize that her body was not then capable of doing what her mind wanted.

If you have chronic stiffness from physical causes, there are two possible solutions. First, you can perform physical exercises to expand your flexibility. The images and exercises that Sally Swift presents in her book *Centered Riding* are very helpful. She uses such techniques as "soft eyes" and breathing exercises to incorporate the feeling of relaxation into the physical aspects of riding. These images may open a window in your mind to a new feeling on horseback.

A second solution may be to recognize that your body can never have the desired flexibility. Instead of becoming discouraged, work with your instructor to find a different position, a different horse, a different set of goals with which you can cope.

Ellie came to me to learn how to jump. But, Ellie had Cerebral Palsy and she could not spread her legs apart. Riding exercises stretched her muscles and allowed her to open her legs a little, but she did not have enough suppleness to jump safely. Finally Ellie was able to face the fact that she would never be a jumper rider. Nevertheless, she recognized the benefits riding had brought her and she pursued a career as a riding instructor. She continues to ride for the physical stretching it offers and for the pleasure it brings.

If you decide that your horse is physically stiff, you should follow a similar approach. First determine if the stiffness is the result of any injury. If it is, consult a veterinarian to learn the extent to which the horse can be worked comfortably. Match your goals for him to his own physical capabilities. Sometimes there is no apparent reason for his stiffness and you can employ the hands-on techniques and exercises of someone like Linda Tellington-Jones to improve his suppleness. A simple technique for a horse with stiff neck muscles is to offer a carrot in your hand which is held near your horse's elbow. He will eagerly stretch his neck muscles while reaching around for the carrot.

Riders may work very hard on their exercise programs and still remain stiff. Their stiffness is not physical in origin, but is caused by mental or spiritual stress. For clarity, I call this kind of stiffness "tension." Stress may be produced by family problems, worry over losing a job, fear of jumping, or trying to own responsibility for too many people's lives. Stress-induced tension may be confused with natural stiffness. Other signals are easily misread or overlooked: Headaches, back aches, inability to move freely, inability to think quickly. All are frequently encountered nuisances that we tend to ignore. Yet, if stresses are too severe or last too long, they can cause permanent damage to the body.

I was a classic case of the effects of generalized stress on the human body. I had had a back problem for many years and I had radiographs to prove that the deterioration was real. Traditional therapy was no help. The fourth therapist I consulted taught me how to relax as part of his treatment. Initially I thought his insistence on relaxation was absurd. Despite my resistance, I could feel the tension leave my body while I was in the relaxation therapy. Although my original doctors had told me to reduce the stress in my life, they never explained to me how the stress was causing the tension and pain in my body. After I realized the connection and had the relaxation therapy, I gradually lost my back pain, although the damage to my spine was permanent.

Discovering that riding problems are really the result of stress-induced tension, may be accidental. John looked like a good rider. His seat was correct and he seemed to follow his horse's rhythm, but his horse always jigged at the walk. John also suffered from extreme sick headaches and eventually I referred him to the therapist who had helped me. When he returned and rode his horse, the horse walked calmly. I attributed the improvement to the horse's rest, but John told me that he felt he could follow the rhythm better and that his sensitivity had improved. Since John's signals were lighter, the horse did not feel like he was in a constant half halt. This experience alerted me to the prevalence of riding problems caused by tension.

Once you understand and accept that your stiffness could be tension you can seek out solutions. Perhaps you need to correct the problems that are causing the stress, or perhaps yoga or some form of meditation will help you to relax. The relaxation therapy that helped me and my riders was developed by Russell Scoop, a physical therapist. He calls it Russell Scoop's Relaxation Therapy (RSRT). I have incorporated RSRT, horse massage and teaching into 5-day clinics.

The results were encouraging for all. One participant said: "I feel much more in touch with my horse and with what my body is doing on the horse." Another said: "For the first time I can feel how tough I am on the horse and how it confuses and angers him. My horse is so much lighter and more correct. At my last show I got my first 60% in dressage." Some of these riders had spent long hours doing physical exercises and being lunged, yet they had made little progress by addressing their stiffness from a purely physical standpoint. The RSRT attacked the underlying mental attitudes and habits that produced the tension originally and the tension gradually lessened.

RSRT is a form of meditation. While you are lying down you take a mental journey through your body, becoming aware of the feelings in each of the parts. Gradually your brain waves slow and your muscles become limp. You remain conscious of your environment, but you feel as though your body is not connected to your mind. This is an extremely important feeling for a rider because you must first be willing to relinquish control over your body before you can totally feel your horse.

The RSRT not only releases generalized muscle tension but it teaches you to identify specific tight spots. One of my riders had very tight shoulders but we were not aware of the severity of the problem until we saw her pouring a bottle of wine. She hunched both shoulders over in the general direction of the glass; she could not move her arms independently of her shoulders. Through RSRT she became aware of the feeling of independence and finally the tensions of twenty years are leaving her body. Her hands and arms are softer and she is better able to communicate with her horse.

A horse probably does not suffer from long-term generalized stress. His simple brain avoids for him the emotional traumas that people are subject to. He might worry if he is taken out of the stable just as the other horses are being fed. However, he will quickly forget his hunger if he is properly handled and given something else to think about. Major fears are reawakened only if the environment is reproduced. As a young horse, Blue had a bad experience with the vet. Each time the vet entered the stable Blue would turn his tail toward the door and not let the vet catch him. However, his owner, a teenage boy, was able to catch him anywhere at any time, even when the vet came. The fear lasted for his entire 22 years with us.

Your spirit is the part of your being that allows for inner-harmony. Inner-harmony can emerge only if you are free from such negative feelings as anger, fear, jealousy, hatred and resentment. Any negative feeling is a stress on your being that causes tension. Identification of the spiritual sources of tension is difficult. Some people seek psychiatric counseling to help them find the source of their negative feelings and repair them. To a large extent the RSRT can help you overcome spiritual stress without even consciously identifying the cause. My own spiritual development was sparked by examining the reasons why the RSRT was so successful. Why did I feel more joy in life? Why could I deal with more problems without panic? Pursuing the answers to these questions led me to realize the interrelationship between body, mind and spirit.

Mental and spiritual relaxation can free your mind of clutter. Without the clutter, you can focus your mind better and handle more variables without feeling overwhelmed. You will feel your horse under you more easily and with more delicacy. Your communications will become more accurate and clearer, so your horse can perform with more freedom. The result will be greater natural beauty. You will use your "imagery" and "mountain top" resources more effectively and will be better able to control your attitudes and emotions. The issues you must consider to make decisions will be clearer. Your more relaxed approach to life will make it easier to unite with your horse.

*Relaxation promotes clear thinking and
allows your intuition to develop. You are more open
to outside stimuli, so you are more aware
of your horse's feelings and movements.
Communications are clearer, lighter and more easily felt.*

When you have learned to cope with your stiffness and tension, you will be a more graceful rider. Your body will move in harmony with the horse's movements, instead of being ahead of or behind the motion. Your legs will breathe in rhythm with the movement in your horse's sides. Your hands will function as though they were part of the horse's mouth. Your seat will remain lightly in the saddle, regardless of your horse's gait. Your relaxed muscles and joints can act as the shock absorbers they were intended to be. Your horse will be more comfortable. You will no longer bounce on his back or grab his mouth, so he won't tense up in anticipation of your hurting him.

The communication between you and your horse is better because neither of you has tense muscles or pain interfering with the flow of messages between the body and the brain. Your legs, seat and hands will only move or resist when they are supposed to, so your horse knows that any activity means business. Even slight pressure with your leg or a shift in weight of your seat bones will be recognized at once by your horse.

What are the benefits of relaxation? Sounder, saner horses and riders are able to give more of themselves. They project more beauty of movement and more athletic ability, give more useful years and experience faster training.

Trust

When your horse trusts you,
he relaxes and accepts whatever you ask.

*T*rust allows you and your horse to perform together without worry about the other's actions. It both promotes relaxation and is the result of relaxation. When you and your horse trust each other, you can do things as a team that either of you might be afraid to do with another partner. A horse will cross a deep river, jump a ditch, or pass a field of pigs because his rider says it is safe, even though all his instincts warn, "danger." You may jump a five foot fence or ride a steep mountain trail because you trust your horse not to do anything foolish.

Before you can trust your horse, you must be able to trust yourself. You will develop trust in yourself as a rider if you carefully plan your riding goals, set reasonable expectations for growth, and recognize your successes in meeting them.

How can your horse trust you? Your horse senses your consistency, love and decisiveness in your daily communications. He relaxes with you. As he comes to trust you, he will do what he thinks you want even if you ask incorrectly.

Appreciation

*Appreciate all dimensions of yourself,
your life and your horse.*

Y ou have a body, mind and spirit, each of which offers
you a unique way to participate in life. If you have maintained their balance and have sought to develop each to its
fullest, you will be ready to enjoy all that you do and feel. You
appreciate the feel of a cool rain on your face or a warm fire,
the challenge of solving a difficult mathematical problem or
of teaching a handicapped child how to ride, and the joy of
prayer or the sense of knowing that you can cope in a difficult
situation.

Your ability to love as described by Paul in First Corinthians: 13 helps you to appreciate everything that happens in
your life. You try to look for good in any person or event. Even
though you recognize the bad things, you do not dwell on

them. You try to accept tragedies as a part of life rather than as a personal failure. You work at keeping the clutter out of your mind so that you can notice the joyful things. You take time out of your busy schedule to smell the flowers or watch the lambs play in the pasture.

Horses offer many opportunities for appreciation. On a very basic level, you can enjoy watching your horse enjoy himself. You should be able to feel your horse's peacefulness and comfort as you watch him sleeping in the spring sunshine. Horses offer companionship, give you a chance to retreat to your "mountain top", and give you a sense of physical exhileration. When you perform together, whether it is in your ring at home, on a ride through the countryside, or in a show, you should feel good each time he does something especially well. These moments may be few and far between — no one can perform perfectly 100% of the time and, anyway, your sense of appreciation would be dulled by a uniformly and continuously excellent performance. But when that moment of excellence occurs, you can be ready to recognize it, reward it, and enjoy it for what it is.

The
Appearance
of
Unity

When you feel at one with your horse,
your image will reveal it.

*T*o yourself in the mirrors, or to another viewing you, you look in harmony with your horse. Your balance is perfect, your timing is accurate, your seat is relaxed and supple, your horse is balanced, obedient, relaxed, yet full of energy, and eager to respond to your requests. Your accomplishment is one of great refinement of physical skills, and the development of mental and spiritual bonding with your horse. You and your horse look and feel as though you are one.

Beyond
the
Mirrors

Introduction

*I*n order for the horse to be revealed in his full natural beauty and for you to appear in complete harmony with his movements, you must have developed a unity of mind and spirit. The level of understanding and communication must be so finely tuned and complete that the differences in physical structure and outlook are no longer apparent. You should experience an inner harmony that is broader than just your own relationship with your horse. It affects your total outlook on life.

Inner-harmony

*I*nner-harmony is like happiness: The harder you look for it, the harder it is to find. You are most likely to find it when you least expect it.

What is inner-harmony? It is an acceptance of yourself, for better and for worse. It is an ability to enjoy the highs in your life and a tranquility to work through the lows without panic or desperation. It is the balance you have achieved between your body, mind and spirit. It is a sense of inner peace, without smugness or egotistical self-praise.

But inner-harmony is not a final arrival which gives you the right to sit back and glory in your accomplishment. One of the wonderful things about people and life is the ever-present opportunity to grow. If life continues on around and without you, you will lose your inner-harmony if you cannot grow with it. However, the knowledge gained of yourself as you journeyed beyond the mirrors will make you aware of the changes needed.

I believe that inner-harmony is a highly personal experience. There are varieties of inner-harmony. Thomas Merton, a Christian mystic, described inner-harmony in terms of an ecstatic experience of oneness with God:

...an emptying of all the contents of the ego consciousness to become a void in which the light of God or the glory of God, the full radiation of the infinite reality of His Being and Love are manifested.

Joe Hyams, a student of Zen might see inner-harmony as a better self:

I feel my life calmer, richer, and fuller. I now have more patience, more tolerance of others, and more self-confidence. I feel myself to be a better father, husband, and friend. I have lost much of the edginess and combativeness that arose from my insecurity. Of course, I would still rather not lose a game, a bid for work, or an argument. But when I do, I can now lose more graciously, accepting defeat as part of the learning process.

Your own answer will be right for you, if you are open and aware enough to recognize your gift of inner-harmony.

Spiritual Unity

S piritual unity between rider and horse is more than the harmonious image seen in the mirror. It is a union of their selves for the benefit of their performance together. The rider is no longer conscious of his own spirit, but only of the bond he has with his horse and of the movements they are performing together.

The effect is similar to that of an actor who totally immerses himself in the role he is playing, or a musician who lets the composer speak through him as he plays. The actor or the musician interprets the role or the music for the audience and, in so doing, loses his own identity into the interpretation.

Achieving spiritual unity uses all of the resources you have accumulated on your journey. True spiritual unity grows out of your inner-harmony. If you still are filled with tensions or uncertainties, you will be unable to free your spirit to join with your horse's. You must be so in tune with yourself that you can function automatically, with your mind floating freely. You no longer have to try to achieve physical harmony with your horse, and, in fact, any effort to do so will interfere with the flow of your mind and block your spiritual unity. You are not afraid of, or embarrassed by, freeing yourself because you know that the identity you form with your horse is, for just that moment, on a higher level than anything you could do on your own.

Natural Beauty

And God said, Let the earth bring forth the living creature after his kind, cattle and creeping thing, and beast of the earth after his kind: and it was so. And God made the beast of the earth after his kind and cattle after their kind, and everything that creepeth upon the earth after his kind: and God saw that it was good.   (Genesis 1:24-25.)

T he horse's beauty, given to him by God, must be maintained. It is not our right to destroy this beauty to create a creature of our own design. Our obligation is to allow the horse to enhance his beauty through our training and our sympathetic riding. As we develop our own inner-harmony and our spiritual unity with the horse, we come to recognize that the horse's full, natural beauty can emerge only with our most tactful, understanding, and patient care. We are the custodians, not the creators, of his beauty.

Beyond the Mirrors

Bibliography

Cather, Willa. *Death Comes for the Archbishop,* Alfred A. Knopf, Inc. 1926.

DeKunffey, Charles. "Concepts of Dressage," *Equestrian Video Library,* Vol. 54, Mercedes Maharis Production.

Hyams, Joe. *Zen in the Martial Arts,* Bantam Books, 1979.

Holy Bible, The. Authorized Version (Otherwise known as the King James Version).

Maltz, Maxwell. *Thoughts to Live By,* Simon & Schuster, 1975.

Merton, Thomas. *Zen and the Birds of Appetite,* New Directions Publishing Corporation, 1968.

Schuller, Robert H.. *Tough Times Never Last, But Tough People Do!,* Bantam Press, 1983.

Suenig, Waldemar. *Horsemanship,* Doubleday & Co., 1956.

Swift, Sally. *Centered Riding,* St. Martin's/Marek, 1985.

Wynmalen, Henry. *Dressage,* A.S. Barnes & Co., 1952.

Other Suggested Reading

Buscaglia, Leo. *Living, Loving & Learning,* Ballantine Books, 1982.

Haich, Elisabeth. *Initiation,* George Allen & Unwin Ltd., 1965.

Humphries, Christmas. *Walk On,* The Buddhist Society, 1947.

Jones, Alan. *Soul Making,* Harper and Row, 1985.